Praise for the Gettysburg Handbook

Don't go to Gettysburg without reading this Insiders' Guide!

"Great book to have before you go to visit Gettysburg."

"Great guide and informative text. A must have for visitors to Gettysburg, regardless of how many times you've been there."

"I rated this highly because every one of the suggested spots that we hit was a real winner. Just great."

"Awesome, Accurate and easy to use!!!!!"

Enjoy Reading Civil War Fiction?

Other Books by Jessica James

AWARD-WINNING WOMEN'S FICTION

LACEWOOD (Dual Era/Civil War)

AWARD-WINNING HISTORICAL FICTION

THE LION OF THE SOUTH

SHADES OF GRAY TRILOGY:

Duty Bound, Honor Bound, Glory Bound

NOBLE CAUSE (Book 1 Heroes Through History)

ABOVE & BEYOND (Book 2 Heroes Through History)

LIBERTY & DESTINY (Book 3 Heroes Through History)

HEROES THROUGH HISTORY BOXED SET (Books 1-3)

AWARD-WINNING ROMANTIC SUSPENSE (Not Civil War)

PRESIDENTIAL ADVANTAGE

DEADLINE (Phantom Force Tactical Book 1)

FINE LINE (Phantom Force Tactical Book 2)

FRONT LINE (Phantom Force Tactical Book 3)

PHANTOM FORCE TACTICAL SERIES SET Books 1-3

PROTECTING ASHLEY

MEANT TO BE: A Novel of Honor and Duty

www.jessicajamesbooks.com

HELP ME KEEP THIS GUIDE UP TO DATE

Every effort is made by the author to make this guide accurate and as useful as possible. However, changes can occur.

I would love to hear from you concerning your experience with this guide and how you feel it could be improved.

You may email me at writefromthepast@yahoo.com with the Subject Line: Gettysburg Handbook

Thank you in advance for your input and Happy Travels to Gettysburg!

Jessica James

Gettysburg
Handbook
And
Insider's Travel Guide

Jessica James

Gettysburg Visitors' Handbook and Insider's Travel Guide
© 2023 by JESSICA JAMES
www.jessicajamesbooks.com

All rights reserved, including the right to reproduce this book, or portions thereof, in any form.

ISBN: 9781941020456

Cover Design by German Creative
Interior Design: Patriot Press

March 2023

Table of Contents

Welcome To Gettysburg!	1
The Best Time To Visit Gettysburg	3
General FAQs About Gettysburg	11
Getting To Gettysburg	12
What To Expect / What To Bring	15
Do's and Don'ts When Visiting Gettysburg	16
Traffic Tip From A Local	17
Public Transportation	18
Brief Summary of the Battle	19
Fast Facts About The Battle	20
Battle of Gettysburg Cannons	21
Civil War Notes	21
How To Explore The Battlefield	23
Bus Tours	23
SegWayTours	23
Battlefield Bike Riding	24
Gettysburg Battlefield Horseback Tours	25
The Best Way To Explore Gettysburg	26
Lincoln And The Gettysburg Address	28
Fast Facts About The Gettysburg Address	29
An Overview of Downtown Gettysburg	31
Gettysburg Museums	38
Don't Miss These Monuments!	42

Not-So-Famous Monuments & Sites	44
Best Kept Secret: Hiding in Plain Sight	52
Is Gettysburg Haunted?	53
Ghost Tours/ Paranormal	64
Romantic Things To Do In Gettysburg	66
Parking in Gettysburg	73
Reenactments in Gettysburg	74
Attending A Reenactment	76
Interesting Places Close By	77
Other Landmarks In Gettysburg	79
Local Special Events	80
Gas Up Before Gettysburg	81
Day Trips From Gettysburg	85
Lesser Known Local Battlefields	86
Where To Eat In Gettysburg	87
Recommended For Historic Value & Food	89
Campgrounds Near The Battlefield	91
The Story of Old John Burns	103
The Battle of Gettysburg:	108
About the Author	117

Introduction

Planning your first trip to Gettysburg?

Or maybe you're a veteran visitor who has been there dozen of times.

Regardless, this book was written to help reveal things you may not know about this historic town and to help steer newcomers toward the things that most interest them.

As a life-long Gettysburg resident, I want to ensure that your trip to Gettysburg is interesting, informative and entertaining—and I also hope that you will be inspired to want to learn more.

Let me be clear... this book is not a complete guide to the town—and it is definitely not a source for history buffs who want to study battlefield tactics.

Rather, this book is designed to answer general questions, provide an overview of the area, and point out things that you won't find anywhere else.

For instance, unlike other Gettysburg Travel Guides, this book tells you things like:

- Where to find the lowest gas prices
- What you can do in Gettysburg for free
- The best times to visit Gettysburg
- Where the locals go to eat
- How to avoid downtown traffic
- What monuments you MUST see for their artistic value
- What monuments you SHOULD see because of hidden stories

I hope I answer ALL of your questions before your visit, but let me make some recommendations as well.

Make sure you visit Destination Gettysburg and the Gettysburg Foundation websites. They both have great itinerary's and up-to-date event calendars for your visit.

I've provided a lot of hints and suggestions for places you might want to explore. You won't find a lot of in-depth details, but you will find hidden gems about things you probably never thought about when planning your trip.

I hope you enjoy reading this book and more importantly, that you have an enjoyable time in Gettysburg.

I do answer my emails. If you have a suggestion – good or bad – feel free to contact me. (writefromthepastATyahoo.com)

Best wishes!

Jessica James

"In a place like Gettysburg, the visitor—the native for that matter—may easily become absorbed in the three days of conflict, forgetting that history was also made here in quiet lives, on farms and village streets, through a century before the battle, through a century after it."

– President Dwight D. Eisenhower

Welcome To Gettysburg!

Your journey starts here...

Gettysburg is a small town of less than 8,000 residents that draws more than a million visitors each year. This number rose to more than three million in 2013 when the 150th anniversary of the Battle of Gettysburg was observed.

The town is a unique blend of past and present, a place where cars and 18-wheelers use the same roads as pedestrians and horse-drawn carriages. For that reason, it's good to have an idea about where you're going and what you want to do before your visit to Gettysburg.

Despite the influx of tourists, Gettysburg maintains its small-town ambiance, with pubs, restaurants, unique shops and boutiques.

Though by no means all-encompassing, this booklet highlights some attractions that are recommended by "a local," as well as information visitors may find useful in getting around and figuring out what to see.

This is not a tour guide to the battlefield, but rather a guide to the town and surrounding area.

There is a plethora of information, maps, guides and tours for those interested in the Battle of Gettysburg and exploring the battlefield.

For the most detailed information and updated event schedule, visit Destination Gettysburg and request a copy of their Visitors Guide.

Another great starting point is the Gettysburg Foundation, which provides up-to-date event information as well as videos of the Battlefield.

This book will help you make your trip to Gettysburg one of the most memorable vacations you will ever take.

If you have limited time, this book is even more important, and if you're on a tight budget, keep reading. There are lots of things to do in Gettysburg that are free.

*****

NOTE THAT IN 2023, LITTLE ROUND TOP IS CLOSED FOR REHABILITATION.

Adams County Statistics

Av. Max. Temperature: 74.8 degrees F

Av. Min. Temperature: 32.2 degrees F

Average Snowfall: 32.2 inches

County Population: 103,852 (2020)

Gettysburg Population: 7,106 (2020)

The Best Time To Visit Gettysburg

Gettysburg is a popular tourist destination, so a common question is "When is the best time to visit Gettysburg?"

The short answer is that there is no one perfect time to visit Gettysburg. Every season has its own unique charms, attractions—and perhaps a few drawbacks.

However, if you're looking for the best combination of weather and events, here is some advice from a local about the best times to visit Gettysburg.

Spring In Gettysburg

Late March through May is one of the best times to visit the Gettysburg battlefield because of the beauty and majesty of spring in southcentral Pennsylvania. Pear trees are planted on most of downtown Gettysburg's sidewalks, and the beauty of the white flowery blooms is truly stunning.

Lincoln Square in downtown Gettysburg is also beautifully landscaped with red and white tulips to make a spectacular splash of color.

Of course, the weather is also warming up, with temperatures ranging from the low 50s to high 70s.

March is an "iffy" month in Gettysburg that can bring lots of rain and wind. On the other hand, it can be just warm enough to be quite comfortable for sightseeing and exploring.

The area surrounding Gettysburg is often neglected by tourists, but apple, peach and cherry tree orchards spread for miles over rolling hills just north and west of town.

When in bloom, the trees provide endless photo opportunities, so if you enjoy taking a drive out into the country and seeing nature's beauty, Spring may be the best time to visit Gettysburg for you.

As the temperatures rise, hotel room rates begin to climb and the tourist attractions get a bit more crowded, but both are still reasonable in the Spring.

Pro Tip: The weather can change from day-to-day and from sunup to sundown, so pack layers of clothing.

The Gettysburg Bluegrass Festival is a key event in both May and August that takes place at the Granite Hill Campground. Some of the biggest names in Bluegrass play over the four-day festival, making these months great times to visit Gettysburg.

Pros Of Visiting Gettysburg In The Spring
- The crowds are thinner
- Weather is cooler and scenery is beautiful for photographs
- Hotels are slightly cheaper

Cons Of Visiting Gettysburg In The Spring
- The weather is unpredictable and can be quite chilly

Visiting Gettysburg In The Summer

Many people think the summer months of June, July and August make the best time to visit the Gettysburg battlefield for a number of reasons.

Peak tourist season in Gettysburg begins in May with many school trips and runs until September when most schools have started again.

Visitors can take advantage of the warmer weather, as well as a wide array of different activities that aren't offered during the other seasons, which is why many people say that summer is the best time to visit Gettysburg.

The anniversary of the Battle of Gettysburg is July 1, 2 and 3 (1863) so the Fourth of July holiday is one of the busiest and most crowded weekends.

Temperatures range from the low 60s to mid-80s and can go well up into the 90s in July and the first part of August.

Many visitors are not aware of how hot and humid Gettysburg can be. The high humidity can make it very uncomfortable for those who do not tolerate heat well (like me), so make sure you stay hydrated and wear comfortable, light clothing.

You will also want to carry plenty of water with you and a good insulated water bottle is a good idea.

If you enjoy hiking and walking the battlefields, then a cooling towel that wraps around your neck is definitely a good idea.

For those who don't mind crowds and warm weather, the summer months are jam-packed with special events and opportunities to witness history.

Civil War historians and living history re-enactors offer demonstrations at the Gettysburg National Park Visitor Center, and The Gettysburg Heritage Center offers special talks and author book signings.

To commemorate the anniversary of the Battle of Gettysburg, a Civil War re-enactment is held at the Daniel Lady Farm each year, which is another reason why summer is considered the best time to visit Gettysburg.

This event features tours of the Lady house and barn, which were both used as Civil War hospitals, as well as lots of demonstrations and activities.

There are many tours in Gettysburg that run throughout the year, but they're more enjoyable on a warm summer evening.

The summer months are also a great time to line up a ghost tour. (Although ghost tours run all year, so don't worry if you're visiting earlier or later in the year).

As far as hotels, you'll want to make your reservations well advance—especially if you want to visit Gettysburg the first week in July. Expect to pay a little more for hotels for this peak season as well.

Pros Of Visiting Gettysburg In The Summer
- The annual Battle of Gettysburg re-enactment
- Lots of living history events through the National Park Service
- Weather is warm

Cons Of Visiting Gettysburg In The Spring
- Weather may be "too" warm
- More crowded than at other times of the year
- Hotel prices are at their peak

Fall Can Be The Best Time To Visit Gettysburg

Many visitors say that their favorite time to visit Gettysburg is the fall months of September, October or November.

The high humidity is gone by this time, and since kids are back in school, the crowds dwindle a bit as well.

The overall weather for exploring is spectacular with temperatures in the high 50s to low 70s and brilliant blue skies.

You can't beat the carnival of color the trees display as they their leaves turn gold, yellow and red in the late fall.

These cooler days make it a great time to book a Gettysburg horseback tour of the battlefield or take a carriage ride through downtown Gettysburg.

Of course, Halloween falls into this time of year and there are plenty of haunted sites to visit in Gettysburg. In fact, it's considered one of the most haunted places in the United States!

You can book a walking ghost tour, a small group ghost investigation or just take a self-guided ghost tour so you can go at your own pace.

In addition, Fall is harvest time. You can find everything from fresh apples, apple cider, pumpkins, wine and farmers markets complete with home-baked items.

Many local orchards also allow you to pick your own fruit.

And perhaps the best time to visit Gettysburg in the Fall is for Remembrance Day Weekend, which is held in November.

Pros Of Visiting Gettysburg In The Fall
- Weather is cool and great for outdoor exploring
- Changing of the leaves makes spectacular vistas
- Less crowded than summer months
- Harvest time and Remembrance Day

Cons Of Visiting Gettysburg In The Fall
- You miss the annual re-enactment

Winter Months in Gettysburg

If you want to plan a visit for December, January or February you will definitely find that crowds are thinner and prices are lower. Gettysburg still makes a wonderful getaway if you don't mind cold weather.

You'll always find an open door at the local pubs and bars to warm up with a hot toddy. There are plenty of other places to get warm in downtown Gettysburg as well, from shops and coffee houses to movie theaters and restaurants.

In some ways, December is one of the best times of year to visit Gettysburg.

The shops offer many one-of-a-kind items that you won't find anywhere else. And the battlefield appears peaceful and serene when it lies under a blanket of snow.

If you're looking for a special event, plan to visit Gettysburg the first weekend in December for the Gettysburg Christmas Festival.

This unique holiday weekend features promotions, games, entertainment, activities and lots of holiday cheer, all wrapped up with Gettysburg's special small-town charm.

If you enjoy being outside during the winter months, then you probably like to ski. You're in luck because Liberty Mountain Resort is less than 10 miles away. They offer skiing, snowboarding and snowtubing slopes.

Pros Of Visiting Gettysburg In The Winter
- You will have a lot of attractions practically to yourself
- Lowest hotel rates
- Skiing and tubing close by
- Christmas in Gettysburg! It only happens once a year!

Cons Of Visiting Gettysburg In The Winter
- Cold weather with a chance of snowy days.
- Some venues may be closed or have reduced hours.

A Tip For A Good Time To Visit Gettysburg

The best time to visit Gettysburg according to many people is the weekend that falls nearest to November 19.

This is called "Remembrance Day Weekend," which commemorates Lincoln's Gettysburg Address and features a magnificent Remembrance Day Parade of re-enactors—both civilian and military—in their Civil War attire.

There are soldiers, horses, women in gowns, children, shopkeepers, preachers, etc. It is truly a sight to see.

Though you may have to brave cold weather, there are many special events that weekend, including Civil War balls, Civil War music being played on the streets and the Gettysburg National Cemetery Illumination.

The Illumination features 3,512 candles placed on the graves of the fallen soldiers at the cemetery. Taps is played in the background and the soldiers' names are read throughout the evening. This is a solemn and unforgettable event.

The temperatures in November can range from cold and sleeting rain to mild temperatures in the 50s. (The weather in November in Gettysburg is unpredictable as the seasons change).

Bring plenty of warm clothes and sip on some hot cider that is sold along the street.

Wrap-Up Of The Best Time To Visit Gettysburg

Gettysburg and the surrounding area is a great place to visit any time of year, but each season has its own unique charm.

The best time to visit Gettysburg really depends on your likes and expectations. No matter when you visit, you'll experience a charming historical town with lots to offer.

General FAQs About Gettysburg

Is the Gettysburg Battlefield free?

Yes, the Gettysburg Battlefield is free. Unlike many other national parks, you can drive anywhere you want on the battlefield roads during daylight hours.

Can you just drive through Gettysburg Battlefield?

Yes, because the battlefield surrounds the town (and is part of the town), it is open to drive or walk through.

Can you tour Gettysburg without a Guide?

Yes, you can tour the battlefield without a guide. There are apps and maps to help guide you, however, Licensed Guides can definitely provide a more in-depth analysis. Battlefield bus tours can provide a great overview if you just want to understand what happened over the three days.

How long does it take to drive through the Battlefield?

Keep in mind that the battlefield encompasses 6,000 acres with more than 26 miles of roads connecting the history landmarks. You can probably drive through it in one day if you don't stop, however the battle took place over 3 days and included fighting in the town. Many of the monuments are in the middle of fields or hidden down forest paths, so getting out and exploring is worthwhile.

How many days do you need for Gettysburg?

Most people recommend three days.

What do I need to know before visiting Gettysburg?

Read this book!

> **DID YOU KNOW?**
>
> Gettysburg was called the "high water mark" of the Confederacy. After that battle, General Lee's army was never able to launch another major offensive.

Getting To Gettysburg

Though a number of highways converge in Gettysburg, the two major routes are U.S. Rt. 30, (east-west), and U.S. Rt. 15, (north-south).

Rt. 30 goes right through downtown (and many other congested downtowns throughout Pennsylvania).

Rt. 15 has six Gettysburg exits. Coming from the South on Rt. 15, you will see them in this order:

Steinwehr Avenue (U.S. Business 15/Emmitsburg Rd.) This exit takes you into the southern end of town (known by locals as the "tourist district.") It is a scenic route through the battlefield (Pickett's Charge) and you will pass the Round Tops.

Taneytown Road (Rt. 134). This is a good exit to take if you are going straight to the battlefield or to the new NPS Visitor Center and Museum. Scenic and not as congested as other routes.

Baltimore Street (Rt. 97). This also brings you into the southern end of town, onto Baltimore St. This exit can also be used for the Visitor Center and for a number of attractions and hotels. The Outlet Shoppes At Gettysburg and a couple of hotels are located right off the exit ramp.

Hanover Street (Rt. 116). This road runs east-west, merges with Rt. 30, and takes you to Lincoln Square/downtown. This road takes you by the historic Daniel Lady Farm, where special events like reenactments are often held during the summer months.

York Street (Rt. 30). This is another east-west route, taking you to Lincoln Square through some unattractive sprawl. There are a number of hotels along this stretch if you're looking for a place to stay within 1 or 2 miles of downtown. Also Gateway Gettysburg Cinemas, Wal-Mart, Sheetz, Beer Mart, State Liquor Store and fast-food restaurants are located right off this exit.

Hunterstown Road (Rt. 394 & U.S. Business Rt. 15). This exit takes you directly to Gettysburg College or to the northern part of Gettysburg, where much of the first day's fighting in the Battle of Gettysburg took place.

Airports:

Gettysburg has a small airport with a 3,100 foot runway.

The closest major airport is Harrisburg International Airport, located about 50 miles away, and the smaller Hagerstown Airport in Hagerstown, Md.

Other airports that are between 90 minutes and 2 hours away are:

Baltimore Washington International, Reagan Washington National and Dulles International.

Excerpt from the 20th Maine Monument Dedication Speech On Little Round Top, 1888

"And reverent men and women from afar, and generations that know us not and that we know not of, heart-drawn to see where and by whom great things were suffered and done for them, shall come to this deathless field, to ponder and dream..."

— Gen. Joshua Lawrence Chamberlain

What To Expect / What To Bring

The temperature statistics can be a little deceiving if you are visiting Gettysburg during the summer months—especially July. It is hot, humid and sticky.

For those of you not familiar with Mid-Atlantic conditions, temperatures in the 90s with high humidity is very uncomfortable.

Wear light-colored clothing and comfortable walking shoes.

Don't forget sun block, sunglasses, hats and water.

In the summer, be prepared for flies during the day and mosquitoes at night.

Also check for deer ticks if walking in high grass.

Dress in layers when traveling in spring, fall or winter. The temperatures are unpredictable.

Do's and Don'ts When Visiting Gettysburg

DO put money in the parking meters in Gettysburg if you don't want to get a ticket. Parking personnel in this town are very diligent!

DO park in the RaceHorse Alley Parking Deck behind the Gettysburg Hotel. (Northeast quadrant of Lincoln Square). Metered spaces on the street are sometimes hard to find.

DO yield to traffic that is already in Lincoln Square, but enter as quickly as possible.

DO check the National Military Park Gettysburg website before your visit to find out what Living History programs and special events are happening.

DON'T dilly-dally in the crosswalks when you're walking. Locals will gladly yield for pedestrians, but one slow walker in Lincoln Square can bring traffic to a halt in the entire town, causing gridlock for blocks in each direction. PLEASE be considerate to those who are trying to drive through town.

DON'T try to read the monuments from the road. Please be courteous and pull to the side so through traffic can pass you.

DON'T plan on picking up a six-pack in Pennsylvania at a gas station. The Commonwealth controls all alcohol sales so you won't find beer and wine in gas stations or convenience stores like other states. (It's complicated).

(See more detailed information in the Adult Beverage section).

Traffic Tip From A Local

If coming from the west on Route 30, look to your left just past the Gettysburg Post office (Rt. 30/Buford Avenue) for an alley BEFORE the traffic signal.

This is RaceHorse Alley, which runs parallel to Rt. 30/Chambersburg Street. The alley will also take you straight to the RaceHorse Ally Parking Garage and to the Gettysburg Hotel without going onto the main streets. This alley is routinely used by locals to bypass the congestion of downtown traffic.

This route is also convenient if you want to turn left onto Washington Street to head north (or visit Gettysburg College) instead of sitting in traffic.

Note: Narrow and prone to potholes.

DID YOU KNOW?

Carrying the flag was a dangerous job, as it often provided an easy target. On one day alone, 23 flag bearers were killed from just two units in Gettysburg.

Public Transportation

Previously known as Freedom Transit, rabbittransit serves Gettysburg in Adams County through four routes: The Lincoln Line, the Blue Line, the Gray Line and the Gold Line.

All lines connect residents and tourists to major destinations throughout the community. Park once and let them do the driving.

There is a new bus station located on Carlisle Street, one block north of Lincoln Square, just one block from the Racehorse Alley Parking Garage.

Uber and Lyft drivers are rare. Check in advance before counting on being able to get a ride.

Brief Summary of the Battle

On July 1: Confederate forces moved into Gettysburg from the west and the north, and drove Union forces back through the streets to Cemetery Hill. During the night, reinforcements arrived for both sides.

On July 2: Lee struck the Union left flank at the Round Tops, Devil's Den, the Wheatfield and the Peach Orchard, and then attacked the Union right at Culp's and East Cemetery Hills. The Federals retained Little Round Top and repulsed the attack on the right.

On July 3: The Confederate infantry was driven from their last grip on Culp's Hill in the morning. In the afternoon, after a preliminary artillery bombardment, Lee attacked the Union center. Pickett's Charge momentarily pierced the Union line but was driven back with severe casualties, resulting in a Union victory for the Battle of Gettysburg.

On July 4: Lee began withdrawing toward Williamsport on the Potomac River. His train of wounded stretched more than 14 miles.

You might want to read about the only battle to take place in two states that happened during the retreat: The Battle of Monterey Pass.

> **DID YOU KNOW?**
>
> *The first battle of the Civil War was at Fort Sumter in South Carolina. Three thousand shells were fired over 38 hours, but not a single man was killed on either side.*

Fast Facts About The Battle

- It began July 1, 1863 & ended July 3, 1863.

- The opposing generals were Major General George Meade and Confederate General Robert E. Lee.

- The battle resulted in up to 51,000 casualties and was considered a Union victory.

- Gen. John Reynolds was the only Union general killed during the battle.

- The Union army came from the South and the Southern army attacked from the North.

- Seven million bullets and artillery shells were fired during battle. (There is a tree limb on display at the Visitor Center that is riddled with bullets).

Battle of Gettysburg Cannons

There are about 380 cannons on the Gettysburg Battlefield. The majority of the cannon tubes are original, but since the carriages were wooden during the Civil War cast iron carriages were created to resemble the artillery units used at Gettysburg.

During the battle, the armies had more than 650 cannons between them. Of the 380 permanently-placed cannons, 14 of the cannon tubes stand upright to mark the headquarters of the major generals participating in the battle.

Of all those cannons now on the battlefield, only one is confirmed to have been used during the Battle of Gettysburg. Cannon Number 253—is located on McPherson Ridge along the Chambersburg Pike.

There is also a 3" ordnance rifle in the George Lomas Center and Museum that was fired during the Battle of Gettysburg. This piece—called "Old Number One"—was captured when Union forces retreated at the end of the day July 1, and was recaptured back at Spotsylvania the following year.

The sound of cannon fire during Pickett's Charge on July 3, was said to have been heard in Pittsburgh.

Civil War Notes

There were almost 6,000 battles and skirmishes during the Civil War. Almost 600 were considered full battles, while about 35 of them were considered major battles.

In 1861, the population of the North was 22 million people. The population of the South was only 9 million people, with 3.5 million of those being enslaved people.

Many "Firsts" During The Civil War

The Civil War introduced many firsts including:

- Medal of Honor (and the first woman MOH recipient)
- Income tax
- Naval torpedoes
- Battlefield photographs
- Repeating rifles
- Snorkel breathing device
- Periscope for trench warfare
- Land mine fields
- Machine guns
- Flame throwers
- Aerial reconnaissance (from balloons)
- First African-American Army Officer

How To Explore The Battlefield

The small town of Gettysburg was the site of the largest land battle ever fought in the Western Hemisphere. If you make the mistake of stopping to ask a local where to find the battlefield, don't be surprised if he puts his finger straight out and spins in a circle.

The Battle of Gettysburg lasted three days, July 1-3, 1863, and the fighting took place all around, and in, the town.

Here are just some of the ways you can explore the town and battlefield:

Bus Tours

GETTYSBURG BATTLEFIELD TOURS
(Battlefield Bus Tours, Jennie Wade House, Ghost Tours)
778 Baltimore Street, Gettysburg
1-877-680-8687

SegWayTours

SEGTOURS
(Visit major historical sites with a Licensed Guide)
22 Springs Avenue, Gettysburg
888-4SEGTOURS

Battlefield Bike Riding

GETTYSBURG BIKE
Bike rentals and supplies.
307 York Street, Gettysburg
717-334-7791

GETTYSBIKE
Battlefield Tours with Licensed Guide if requested.
Official season April 20-Oct. 31. Others by request.
Located in the Bus and RV lot at the Visitor Center,
1195 Baltimore Pike, Gettysburg
Reservations: reservations@gettysbike.com

BICYCLE MAPS

If you're bringing your own bike and you just need maps. Tailored to bikers who want to learn history as they ride.

GETTYPEDS
Battlefield tours and rentals on electric bike.
Veteran and family owned. Seasonal.
71 Buford Avenue, Gettysburg
717-398-2600

Gettysburg Battlefield Horseback Tours

If you want to take a Gettysburg Battlefield Tour on Horseback, here are a few options.

HICKORY HOLLOW FARM
Scenic Trail Rides or Tours with Licensed Guides
717-334-0349

ARTILLERY RIDGE
(Campground with horse park. Stalls for your horse).
610 Taneytown Rod, Gettysburg
717-334-1288

CONFEDERATE TRAILS
(Also offers carriage rides and Licensed Guides)
717-476-7428

BATTLEFIELD TOUR WITH A LICENSED GUIDE

You can hire a licensed guide to take you around in your own vehicle. Customized for your interests.
717-337-1709
gettysburgtourguides.org

What is the Best Way To Explore Gettysburg?

Since I'm from Gettysburg, people often ask for a recommendation on what is the best way to see the battlefield.

The answer is impossible for me to say, because it depends on how much time you have and what your interests are.

My first choice would be horseback, but that's just because I love being in a saddle any chance I get. For most people, I doubt that sitting on a hot sweaty horse when it's 95 degrees is their idea of a good time. (Not to mention that you will probably be sore for days afterward from using muscles you didn't know you had).

If you're really into the details of the battle, or want to hear in-depth stories about tactics and the Civil War period, your best bet is to hire a Licensed Guide to show you around.

Another benefit of a Guide is that they can concentrate on what your interests are and spend more time on those topics. (If you're just interested in one day of the battle, they can show you that. If you want to get a good overview of the entire three days, they can hit all of the main points).

If you have limited time and want to get a general overview, you should check out a bus tour. (Double-decker buses are fun for families with kids).

If you want to take your time and be able to get out and walk around, then the self-guided tour is your best bet. (Keep in mind that the battlefield is 6,000 acres with 24 miles of roads, so getting lost is easy to do).

If you have time to do any walking or bike riding (or Segway), I highly recommend it because there is so much you won't see from a vehicle.

Explore The Town Of Gettysburg

At the opening of the Civil War, Gettysburg was a typical northern community made up of English, German, Irish, and African-Americans of various economic and cultural backgrounds.

But in July 1863, Gettysburg's citizens found themselves at the center of a battle.

In addition to the suffering they underwent during the fighting, the townspeople endured terrible hardships for months afterward. They opened their houses to the wounded, provided medical assistance, and helped bury the dead.

As was included in one report: "The surrounding countryside too was part of 'one vast hospital.'"

The civilian stories of the town—and the buildings that still bear the scars of battle—are as interesting as those of the battlefield.

The labor of citizens in caring for the suffering mass of humanity persuaded the editor of The Sentinel that "when the history of this war is written by future historians the Christian charity of the people of Gettysburg would not be forgotten."

DOWNTOWN WALKING TOUR

There are lots of Gettysburg Town Tours available, starting at 11 Lincoln Square. Phone: (443) 324-1936

There are many different tours to choose from including:
Civilian Experiences
Seldom Seen Sites
Presidential History
Black History
Historic Taverns
Unsolved Mysteries

Lincoln And The Gettysburg Address

President Abraham Lincoln arrived in Gettysburg by train on November 18, 1863, after being invited by David Wills to say a few appropriate remarks at the dedication of the national cemetery.

The historic train station also served as a field hospital during the Battle of Gettysburg, transporting 15,000 wounded soldiers after the battle.

The Train Station has been beautifully restored. It is now a Virtual Reality experience run by the Gettysburg Foundation.

Ticket to the Past - Unforgettable Journeys

35 Carlisle St., Gettysburg

The Wills House

After arriving at the station, Lincoln walked up Carlisle Street to the David Wills house on Lincoln Square. Built circa 1816, the house is one of the oldest structures in Gettysburg.

Renovated and opened in 2009, the Wills House tells the story of a town recovering from the devastation of battle, and a war-worn President who came to dedicate a national cemetery.

The museum includes six galleries, including the famous bedroom where Lincoln finished revising the Gettysburg Address.

Limited hours so check before you go.
8 Lincoln Square

www.davidwillshouse.org

Fast Facts About The Gettysburg Address

The Gettysburg Address contains 10 sentences and lasted about two minutes. The final sentence accounts for almost a third of the speech.

The leading orator of the day, who spoke for two hours before Lincoln, wrote to him afterward and said, "Sir, I should be grateful to flatter myself that I came as near to the central idea of the occasion in two hours, as you did in two minutes."

The Gettysburg Address is now regarded as one of the best speeches in U.S. history.

The Gettysburg Address

ABRAHAM LINCOLN

Four score and seven years ago our fathers brought forth on this continent, a new nation, conceived in Liberty, and dedicated to the proposition that all men are created equal.

Now we are engaged in a great civil war, testing whether that nation, or any nation so conceived and so dedicated, can long endure. We are met on a great battle-field of that war. We have come to dedicate a portion of that field, as a final resting place for those who here gave their lives that that nation might live. It is altogether fitting and proper that we should do this.

But, in a larger sense, we can not dedicate—we can not consecrate—we can not hallow—this ground. The brave men, living and dead, who struggled here, have consecrated it, far above our poor power to add or detract. The world will little note, nor long remember what we say here, but it can never forget what they did here. It is for us the living, rather, to be dedicated here *to the unfinished work which they who fought here have thus far so nobly advanced.*

It is rather for us to be here dedicated to the great task remaining before us—that from these honored dead we take increased devotion to that cause for which they gave the last full measure of devotion—that we here highly resolve that these dead shall not have died in vain—that this nation, under God, shall have a new birth of freedom—and that government of the people, by the people, for the people, shall not perish from the earth.

An Overview of Downtown Gettysburg

A trip to the Gettysburg Battlefield is not complete without exploring historic downtown Gettysburg, PA.

After all, it's part of the battlefield too. Fighting took place on the streets and the wounded were treated in every church, house and barn that could take them in.

Downtown Gettysburg offers a diverse array of restaurants, bars, unique shops and one-of-a-kind boutique hotels for every taste.

Lots Of Options In Downtown Gettysburg

Gettysburg, Pennsylvania is known for its rich history, its charming small town atmosphere, and its hospitality. There's something about strolling down brick-paved sidewalks that transports you to another time.

Because Gettysburg is so walkable, businesses that are located on Steinwehr Avenue and Baltimore Street are included on this list, even though they aren't technically "downtown."

(The distance between downtown Gettysburg and the more touristy district of Steinwher Avenue is a little more than a mile).

If you like to park the car and walk instead of searching for a parking space, you can stay in a hotel on Steinwehr Avenue and walk to the downtown area.

Likewise, you can stay in downtown Gettysburg and walk to the restaurants and shops on Steinwehr Avenue.

Either way, walking is probably easier than finding parking.

Metered street parking is available in downtown Gettysburg,

but sometimes hard to come by. There is a parking deck at 74 East Racehorse Alley behind the Gettysburg Hotel, which sits on the northeast side of Lincoln Square.

Downtown Gettysburg Restaurants

Whether you're craving a simple ice cream cone, a slice of pizza or a romantic candlelight dinner, downtown Gettysburg has something for you.

Here are a few of the options you have to grab a bite to eat in downtown Gettysburg.

Pro Tip: You can go on a downtown Foodie Tour to get a taste of Gettysburg!

AMERICAN FARE

One Lincoln: 1 Lincoln Square, Gettysburg. Variety of fresh salads, sandwiches and entrées.

The Pub: 20-22 Lincoln Square. Wonderful place to sit and people-watch. Great menu. Nice bar area if you just want to grab a quick bite.

GRAB A SANDWICH

Lincoln Diner: 32 Carlisle St., Gettysburg, Pa. Everyone goes here. (Great desserts)!

Gettysburg Baking Company: 17 Lincoln Square. Homemade bread, desserts and yummy sandwiches. Mostly to go. Only a few tables.

Hunt's Battlefield Fries: 61 Steinwehr Avenue, Gettysburg. A local and visitor favorite for a quick bite to eat.

PIZZA

Antica Napoli: 39 N. Washington St. This is a hidden little gem tucked in between a laundromat and flower shop. Turn north one block west of the square. Turn into parking lot BEFORE railroad tracks to back of building.

Mama Ventura's: 13 Chambersburg St. Nice sit down Italian food and pizza. Bar down below.

WINGS AND BURGERS

Blue and Gray Bar and Grill: 2 Baltimore St., Gettysburg. Large bar, varied menu. Great wings and sandwiches.

The Gettysburger Company: 35 Chambersburg St., Gettysburg. Hand-pressed pure beef burgers. (They're big)!

BIT OF IRISH

Garryowen Irish Pub: 126 Chambersburg St., Gettysburg

O'Rorke's Eatery & Spirits: 44 Steinwehr Avenue, Gettysburg. Not in downtown, but close to everything in the tourist district. A favorite among reenactors. Outdoor seating in the summer.

CHINESE FOOD DOWNTOWN

ChinaTown Kitchen: 25 York St., Gettysburg. Well-liked by locals. Long-time establishment. Only a few tables so plan to takeout.

Li's Buffet: 165 York St., Gettysburg. Also a place where locals go. Lots of choices in their buffet.

ICE CREAM

Mr. G's Ice Cream: 44 Baltimore St., Gettysburg. A favorite both locals and out-of-towners.

Pro Tip: If you go to Mr. G's, make sure you check one of the witness trees that was standing during the Battle of Gettysburg.

Sunset Ice Cream Parlor: 33 Steinwehr Ave., Gettysburg. Old-fashioned ice cream parlor. Lots of fun and delicious.

BARS ON LINCOLN SQUARE

The restaurants that are right on the square and have bars include:

The Pub: 20 Lincoln Square, Gettysburg.

Blue and Gray: 2 Baltimore St., Gettysburg.

One Lincoln: One Lincoln Square, Gettysburg.

Ploughman Cider Taproom: 16 Lincoln Square, Gettysburg.

There are lots of other bars on the streets surrounding the square and on Steinwehr Avenue. A local favorite is the Reliance Mine Saloon on Steinwehr Avenue.

Flying Bull Bar: Local hang-out ½ block from Lincoln Square
28 Carlisle Street

Gary Owen Irish Pub: Popular with locals. 2 blocks from square.
126 Chambersburg St.

DOWNTOWN GETTYSBURG SHOPS

There are plenty of places to choose from if you're thinking about a downtown Gettysburg shopping excursion. These are just a few of the Gettysburg stores you can find within a block of Lincoln Square.

Lark Gifts: 17 Lincoln Square. One of the most popular gift shops in Gettysburg, with a wide variety of home decor, soaps, jewelry, and even candy. Fun shopping experience in downtown Gettysburg!

The Antique Center of Gettysburg: 30 Baltimore St., Gettysburg. Like a museum even if you're not in the market for anything.

Union Cigar Shop: 5 Baltimore St., Gettysburg.

Sweet (Candy Shop): 100 Baltimore St., Gettysburg.

Gallery 30: 30 Chambersburg St., Gettysburg. Lots of handcrafted American goods.

Adams County Winery: 17 Lincoln Square. Wine made in Adams County, Pa.

Dirty Billy's Hats: 20 Baltimore St., Gettysburg. Unique handmade hats properly fitted.

The Christmas Haus: 13 Baltimore St., Gettysburg. It's Christmas all year here.

A&A Village Treasures: 53 Chambersburg St., Gettysburg. Variety of gifts and clothing.

Other Shopping In Gettysburg

Within one block in each direction of the square there are other Gettysburg stores, including a shoe store, numerous women's clothing boutiques, handmade soap and a variety of other shops and businesses.

Shopping Near Downtown Gettysburg

If Outlet Malls are more your style, Gettysburg has you covered there too. The Outlet Shoppes are located less than three miles south of downtown Gettysburg on Baltimore Street/Route 97.

Downtown Gettysburg Hotels (Just a few)

Gettysburg Hotel: 1 Lincoln Square, Gettysburg. Iconic hotel on the square. Walk to everything. Haunted.

1863 Inn of Gettysburg: 516 Baltimore St., Gettysburg, Pa. Close to everything, midway between tourist district and downtown Gettysburg.

The Federal Pointe Inn: 75 Springs Avenue, Gettysburg, Pa. Close to a shopping center. Has a small bar and restaurant. Historic building that was once a school.

Inn At Cemetery Hill: 613 Baltimore St., Gettysburg. Located in the heart of the tourist district and .6 miles from downtown Gettysburg.

Of course there aren't just hotels in downtown Gettysburg. You can also find a wide variety of Bed and Breakfast Inns that provide both history and hospitality. In fact, The Gettysburg Academy B&B is one of the town's oldest buildings, and is just two blocks from downtown Gettysburg.

FAQ's

Is Gettysburg Walkable?

Yes. Gettysburg is very walkable. From the downtown area to the tourist district on Steinwehr Avenue is only about a mile.

Is Gettysburg Walkable At Night?

As a local, I would feel safe walking in Gettysburg at night. Like anywhere else though, you should always be aware of your surroundings.

Is Gettysburg Dog Friendly?

Many of the businesses in downtown Gettysburg are dog

friendly, as are many of the hotels. (See www.pastlanetravels.com for a list of dog-friendly hotels).

Wrap-Up Of Things To Do In Downtown Gettysburg

Gettysburg has a bustling downtown with plenty of options for dining, shopping, and entertainment.

Restaurants offer a wide range of cuisines, from bar grub to fine dining. The shopping scene is equally diverse, with a mix of boutiques, souvenir shops and stores that sell hats, shoes and even cigars.

For those looking to unwind after a busy day, there are plenty of bars and pubs to choose from. And for those who need a place to stay, there are several hotels, ranging from budget-friendly options to luxurious accommodations.

Whether you're in town for business or pleasure, or want to explore history or just relax, downtown Gettysburg offers something for everyone.

Gettysburg Museums

Not a complete list, but a diverse one.

BEYOND THE BATTLE MUSEUM: Operated by the Adams County Historical Society that covers the county from prehistoric days to modern times. Includes lots of artifacts, interactive displays for children and an immersive exhibit that highlights the civilian experience during the Battle of Gettysburg.
625 Biglerville Road, Gettysburg, Pa.
717-334-4723

AMERICAN HERITAGE CENTER: This museum is worth the stop for the unique displays with a town setting and a large gift shop.
297 Steinwehr Avenue, Gettysburg, Pa.
717-334-6245

GENERAL LEE'S HEADQUARTERS: Free but only open on special occasions. A short interpretive trail is open dawn to dusk.
www.battlefields.org
401 Buford Avenue, Gettysburg, Pa.
717-334-3141

GETTYSBURG DIORAMA: More than 20,000 hand-painted miniatures gives you a great overview of the battle in a 35-minute program.

241 Steinwehr Avenue, Gettysburg, Pa.
717-334-6408

GETTYSBURG MUSEUM OF HISTORY: Civil War, Political and World War artifacts exhibited in an old style museum setting. FREE.
219 Baltimore Street
717-337-2035

JENNIE WADE HOUSE MUSEUM: Wade was the only civilian killed during the battle. A memorable story and experience. (Recommended as a great civilian story).
www.gettysburgbattlefieldtours.com
548 Baltimore Street, Gettysburg, Pa.
717-334-4100

LINCOLN TRAIN MUSEUM: Simulated train ride with Lincoln and 1,000's of model trains. (Must see for train enthusiasts).
425 Steinwehr Avenue, Gettysburg, Pa.
717-334-5678

NATIONAL PARK VISITOR CENTER AND CYCLORAMA: Large Visitor and Museum as well as well-stocked gift shop and book store. Great place to get oriented, buy tickets and prioritize your visit. The Cyclorama painting is recommended by many. Fairly long walk from parking lots. Picnic tables and shade available.
1195 Baltimore Pike (Rt. 97), Gettysburg, Pa.
717-338-1243

THE SHRIVER HOUSE: Great place to understand the impact of war on civilians. (Highly Recommend)
309 Baltimore St., Gettysburg, Pa.
717-337-2800

SEMINARY RIDGE MUSEUM: A modern museum in the heart of the first day of fighting. Historically famous cupola can be visited.
61 Seminary Ridge, Gettysburg, Pa.
717-339-1300

WWII AMERICAN EXPERIENCE MUSEUM: Museum that features artifacts and displays of the World War II era, highlighting the American Experience. Lots of hands-on things to do for kids and special events.
845 Crooked Creek Road, Gettysburg, Pa.
717-253-3414

CHILDREN OF GETTYSBURG 1863: Gives young visitors a hands-on history experience through the stories of the children who lived there during and after the Battle.
451 Baltimore St., Gettysburg, Pa.
877-874-2478

EISENHOWER NATIONAL HISTORIC SITE: Located adjacent to the Gettysburg Battlefield. Tour the President's home or enjoy a self-guided walk around the farm.
Entrance off Emmitsburg Road, passed W. Confederate Ave.
717-338-9114

CIVIL WAR TAILS DIORAMA MUSEUM: Located in the Old Homestead Orphanage, this unique museum features miniature cats as soldiers in their dioramas.
785 Baltimore Street, Gettysburg, Pa.
717-420-5273

MUSEUM OF HAUNTED OBJECTS: The name says it all. It is Spooky!
242 Baltimore Street, Gettysburg, Pa.
717-338-1818

Suggestions For Things Free Things To Do

When you don't have time to see everything and you don't have much money.

- Watch the sunset from Little Round Top. It's spectacular! NOTE: Little Round Top is closed for rehabilitation through 2023.

- Explore Devils Den. You can't see everything from the road. Park the car and walk around.

- Few tourists ever see the mural at Coster Avenue on East Stevens St. Extension. This 80-foot wall mural depicts Confederate troops of Colonel Isaac Avery breaching the defensive line of the 154th New York on the same ground where the action took place in 1863. (From Lincoln Square: Carlisle St., north to Stevens St. Turn right and go straight).

- Sachs Mill Bridge. Located off Pumping Station Road, this bridge was used by both Union and Confederate troops during the Civil War. One of two covered bridges in Adams County—this one is a favorite for ghost hunters.

- Window shop on Steinwehr Ave. There are many "touristy" stores here, but also some high quality shops, eateries, and places to just sit and people watch. Park and go for a stroll.

- Don't forget to walk around downtown. Some of the best shopping can be found within one block in each direction of the square. Also lots of restaurants and bars.

- Climb one of the towers to get a panoramic view: Oak Hill, Culp's Hill or Longstreet's Tower on Confederate Avenue.

- Look for artillery shells still lodged in buildings. (See Not-So-Famous Sites).

Don't Miss These Monuments!

There are 1,328 memorials, monuments and plaques (and 400 cannons) on the Gettysburg Battlefield. You won't have time to see them all -- but here a few that you shouldn't miss.

Pennsylvania: Largest monument on the battlefield, with a viewing area at the top. South of the high-water mark on Hancock Avenue.

Virginia: Imposing, captivating. Located along Confederate Avenue. Lots of cannons on this road and "witness trees." Great view of the Round Tops. (The next three monuments are also on Confederate Avenue).

North Carolina: Life-like image of Confederates rushing to the front. Confederate Avenue. Awe-inspiring. Located on Confederate Avenue.

Louisiana: Beautiful. Angel overlooking dying soldier. Confederate Avenue.

Mississippi: Beautiful, yet shows the violence of war. Depicts fallen color-bearer, with comrade stepping over his body, using his musket as a club to defend the fallen flag.. Confederate Avenue.

General Warren: A lesser known hero, but well known monument. Engineer who saw the importance of gaining control of Little Round Top. Stands on Little Round Top.

Eternal Peace Light Memorial: On Mummasburg Road, north of Gettysburg. Dedicated during 75th anniversary of the Battle of Gettysburg.

Friend to Friend Masonic Memorial: The Masonic Memorial is on the south side of Gettysburg in the National Cemetery Annex off Taneytown Road at the intersection with Steinwehr Avenue. (Can see from Tommy's Pizza parking lot). Depicts Union Captain Henry Bingham, a Mason and staff assistant to General Hancock rendering aid to the fallen Confederate General Armistead, a close friend of Hancock.

Not-So-Famous Monuments & Sites

BABY BIRDS:

This monument is on Doubleday Avenue on Oak Ridge and is one of my absolute favorites.

Location: If you visit the Eternal Peace Light Memorial, exit left and take an immediate right. It is the tall white monument on your left.

This tribute to the 90th Pennsylvania Infantry features a highly-detailed tree made of granite.

The bark of the tree trunk is stripped in areas and splintered on the side from a grazing shot. The trunk itself is shattered at the top, with the cannonball that caused it still embedded in the tree's heart.

But nestled on the remaining stub of a branch is a mother bird feeding two babies.

According to legend, a Confederate cannonball did hit a tree near the regiment and knocked a bird's nest to the ground. A soldier replaced the nest back up in the tree, which gave the veterans an idea for their monument in Gettysburg.

Others have a different theory, saying that the tree symbolizes a nation shattered by war, but the scars are healing and there are signs of new life among the ruins.

Either way, it's a beautiful monument that doesn't get a lot of attention.

SALLIE THE DOG:

Location: This monument is just a little farther down from Baby Birds/Tree monument.

This monument to the 11th Pennsylvania Volunteers stands in a row of Union monuments and features an infantry soldier standing on top a granite base. (Look for the tall monument with an Eagle on top. The soldier is about two monuments farther).

You'll only see Sallie if you stop and walk around to the front of the monument. Sallie was a pit bull terrier that became a mascot for the 11th Pennsylvania.

She was reported to have taken position during the Battle of Gettysburg and barked furiously at the Confederate Army.

Sallie didn't die until 1865 during the Battle of Hatcher's Run, but when the monument was being created, the men of the 11th Pa. wanted to include her.

Sallie is one of two dogs memorialized on the Gettysburg battlefield. The other one is perhaps more famous because it is located near the road. It's an Irish Wolfhound on the Irish Brigade monument near The Wheatfield.

> **DID YOU KNOW?**
>
> *The Civil War lasted 1,396 days, from 1861 until 1865. Approximately 623,000 soldiers died in 10,455 military "events."*

THE HATCHET:

You won't see the hatchet on the 13th Vermont monument unless you're looking for it.

The monument shows features Lt. Stephen Brown who was disciplined for allowing his soldiers to stop for water, and his sidearm was taken.

He ended up going into battle with nothing but a camp hatchet, and during Pickett's Charge, he captured a Confederate officer "at hatchet point."

When the 13th Vermont requested to Brown on top of their monument with the hatchet, park officials nixed the idea.

But the veterans got the last laugh because if you go to the 13th Vermont and look closely, the edge of the hatchet can be seen at the base of Brown's feet.

Location: Hancock Avenue.

WAR GRAFFITI:

Graffiti Is kind of a bad word, especially in the historical world, but in this case, it's very interesting.

There are a number of engravings and carvings left by Civil War soldiers in Gettysburg, but you have to look very hard to find them.

One of them is the McPherson Barn along Meredith Avenue. This site is only open on special occasions, but if you get to visit, make sure you look for the carvings in the stone above the first-floor window of some Civil War veterans who returned years after the battle.

There are also carvings in the barn at the Daniel Lady farm that were left by veterans. (This is where the annual re-enactment is held). Full story on this Civil War hospital.

There are others around the Gettysburg battlefield, including the "DA" rock to mark David Acheson's grave, the Strong Vincent rock on Little Round Top, and the Coble Rock at the base of Culp's Hill.

MISIDENTIFIED SOLDIER:

After the Battle of Gettysburg, the remains of a soldier were found and believed to be that of J.L. Johnson with the 11th Massachusetts. He was buried among fellow Union soldiers in the Massachusetts plot in Soldiers' National Cemetery.

It was later discovered that there was no J.L. Johnson in that regiment. There was, however, a J.L. Johnson in the 11th Mississippi who was killed and never recovered.

It is suspected that Johnson's headboard was misread. If that is correct, he would be the only Confederate buried in the cemetery.

NOT IN THE FIGHT:

The men of the 84th Pennsylvania performed their duties as part of the Union Army's Third Corps, and therefore believed they deserved a monument in Gettysburg.

In reality, they spent the duration of the three-day battle guarding wagon trains in Westminster, Md., almost 25 miles away.

Their monument stands just north of the Pennsylvania Memorial at the corner of Pleasanton and Hancock Avenues.

WITNESS TREES:

There are a number of trees in Gettysburg that "witnessed" both the Battle of Gettysburg and Lincoln's processions through town.

Two of them area giant Sycamores along Baltimore Street. One is in front of Mr. G's Ice Cream (across from the Farnsworth House), and the other is a block away.

There are also trees on Confederate Avenue and in the Soldiers National Cemetery.

ARTILLERY SHELLS IN BUILDINGS:

You might want to do a search before your visit to find out where you can see artillery shells and cannon balls still lodged in buildings.

Here are a few you can look for:

Downtown next to the Wills House on York Street. Above the word "ICE" in Ice Cream, below the second story window.

Another can be seen fairly clearly lodged in the brick of the Old Academy Bed and Breakfast on High Street.

There is a cannon ball embedded in a private brick home on Baltimore street across from Breckinridge Avenue, and there are two projectiles found on Stratton Street, almost opposite each other protruding from privately owned houses beyond the railroad tracks.

There is a shell lodged the Shead's House, which is located across from the Lutheran Seminary grounds on Buford Avenue at the bottom of the hill. The house is painted gray brick with gingerbread awning below the roof. The unexploded shell can be seen to the left of the top window below the awning.

Another shell can be seen in a house on the Lutheran Seminary campus. It was owned by the Seminary president who was an ardent abolitionist. He was on the list for men to capture when the Confederates invaded Gettysburg. Although he successfully evaded capture, the enemy ransacked his house and destroyed much of the Seminary. There is a cannonball embedded in the wall on the porch near the door and under the protruding roof.

PRESIDENTIAL PEWS

Even though Gettysburg is a small town, more than two dozen Presidents have paid the town a visit. In 1863, Abraham Lincoln came for a day, and after delivering his Gettysburg Address, he attended a church service.

His pew is preserved at the Gettysburg Presbyterian Church on the corner of Baltimore and High streets. Two other Presidents attended that church as well, and their pews are also marked: Dwight D. Eisenhower, who lived in Gettysburg after his presidency; and Richard Nixon, who attended Easter service with the widowed Mamie when he was serving as the 37th President of the United States.

50-STAR FLAG

At the same Presbyterian Church, there is a unique artifact preserved in glass in the entryway. General Eisenhower, who was also the 34th president of the United States, purchased his Gettysburg farm in 1950. Because he presided over the nation when Alaskan and Hawaii became states in 1959, he was given the first 50-star United States banner.

The flag was then donated to the church he attended while in Gettysburg.

STAINED GLASS WINDOW

If you happen to attend church service at St. Francis Catholic Church on High Street, make sure you take notice of the beautiful stained glass windows.

Memorialized in the glass are the Sisters of Charity, nuns from nearby Emmitsburg, Md., who rushed to Gettysburg to aid the wounded.

CAMP LETTERMAN

In the midst of the sprawl of that greets visitors when arriving in Gettysburg from the East, you will see a single inconspicuous monument that memorializes Camp Letterman, the largest tented hospital site during the entire Civil War.

By the time Camp Letterman shut down, more than 15,000 Union soldiers and 6,800 Confederate soldiers received treatment.

Unfortunately, more than 1,200 soldiers died from their wounds, infection or disease at the site.

Camp Letterman stood across from the present-day McDonald's and encompassed all of the area that is currently strip malls and businesses.

A Civil War hospital and barn were also torn down to build the Wal-Mart located on the other side of Route 30/York Road.

Best Kept Secret: Hiding in Plain Sight

If you know about "Penelope," you probably know more than 90 percent of Gettysburg residents!

This Gettysburg historical site couldn't be more obvious—yet hardly anyone knows about it (even locals)

Embedded in the sidewalk on the east side of Baltimore Street between Middle and High streets, is a small artillery piece that is a relic from the War of 1812, named Penelope. (Look for the Wayside Exhibit sign in front of a brick house)

The cannon was used during the War of 1812 to announce American victories, and remained in use after the war for Fourth of July celebrations. But in 1855, too much gunpowder was used during an election causing the cannon to partially explode.

The editor of the Gettysburg newspaper at the time—Henry Stahle—wanted to keep the cannon so he kept her chained in front of his office on Baltimore St.

That's where Penelope was when the Battle of Gettysburg raged through the streets in July of 1863, and when President Lincoln passed by on his way to deliver his Gettysburg Address.

And that's where Penelope remains today. From a time when the road was dirt to a paved main street and sidewalks, Penelope remains as a tangible link to the past.

Is Gettysburg Haunted?

Gettysburg became famous for the horrific three-day battle that took place in and around the town in 1863, so it's little wonder that there are lost souls still wandering in between worlds.

There are hundreds, if not thousands, of reported supernatural sightings in Gettysburg as a result of the bloody conflict that left more than 51,000 causalities. Dead and dying men filled the streets and every house, church, barn and building within miles.

If you'd prefer to get spooked by going on a haunted Gettysburg walking tour or even an actual ghost hunting investigation in one of Gettysburg's haunted buildings, then read the next section on Ghost Tours.

Whether you love being scared—or you're just curious about the local lore of one of America's most famous haunted towns—keep reading to learn more about the most haunted places in Gettysburg.

Where Are Gettysburg's Most Haunted Places?

Gettysburg was witness to an incomprehensible amount of suffering and death during three days in 1863 and beyond.

But the most haunted places in Gettysburg aren't just on the battlefield.

Bars, B&B's and even restaurants and hotels are known for their supernatural activity in this historic small town.

You don't have to go on a ghost tour to get spooked in this town. So grab a partner, get your ghost hunting gear ready and prepare for a scare!

The Daniel Lady Farm

If you're looking for proof of a horrific battle, then you need look no further than this stone house and its accompanying barn. Both buildings were used as part of a field hospital after the Battle of Gettysburg.

Evidence of the horrors of the battle remain in the bloodstains on the floor of the house, as well as the engraved initials of wounded soldiers in the door jamb of the barn.

For some history of the farm and pictures of the bloodstains in the house (which were tested and proven to be human blood) see the post The Daniel Lady Farm.

When you see inside the house, you will see why the Daniel Lady Farm is among the most haunted places in Gettysburg.

According to records, at least 37 soldiers who died at the farm were buried on the grounds. Twenty-two of those were not able to be identified, so their families never knew what happened to them.

The Daniel Lady Farm is now owned by the Gettysburg Battlefield Preservation Association and is open for special events and tours of the house.

The historic Lady Farm is located just east of Gettysburg at 1008 Hanover Road (Rt. 116) Gettysburg.

The Tillie Pierce Inn

This haunted house is now a Bed and Breakfast Inn, so book a night if you want to ghost hunt without leaving your room.

This was the home of 15-year-old Tillie Pierce, who became an unlikely heroine in 1863 when she and other local residents were trapped in town during the Battle of Gettysburg.

> **DID YOU KNOW?**
>
> For every man who died from battle wounds inflicted in the war, two died from disease.

Lucky for us, Tillie kept a journal which was made into a book, giving everyone an idea of what the town's people endured. Even though she was just a teenager, Tillie dressed wounds, carried water and tried to comfort the wounded.

She says in her journal:

"Nothing before in my experience had ever paralleled the sight we then and there beheld. There were the groaning and crying, the struggling and dying, crowded side by side, while attendants sought to aid and relieve them as best they could...."

The "Blue Room" is said to be haunted by soldiers who were once treated by Tillie. Guests say they hear footsteps marching through the halls and in the attic above.

Other guests have seen troops wandering up and down the stairs as if on patrol, and one guest was frightened when they opened their door and saw a ghost sitting on the edge of their bed.

The Tillie Pierce House is located at 301 Baltimore Street, Gettysburg, PA.

Jennie Wade House

Often referred to as America's scariest haunted house, the Jennie Wade House is the site of the only civilian death during the Battle of Gettysburg.

Jennie Wade was hit by a stray bullet as she stood baking in the kitchen, and was killed instantly.

Visitors often hear loud bangs and feel sudden rushes of cold air when on the second floor of the Jennie Wade House.

You can't help but get an eerie feeling when you are taken down to the small, cramped cellar where the family was forced to sit with Jennie's body waiting for the shooting to stop.

House tours are available as well as after-hour ghost tours.

The Jennie Wade House is located 548 Baltimore Street, Gettysburg, PA 17325.

The Cashtown Inn

The Cashtown Inn is one of the most famous historical buildings around Gettysburg, and has also gained fame for being one of the most haunted places in Gettysburg.

Built in 1797 and soon used as a tavern and boarding inn, the Cashtown Inn became the first stage coach stop west of Gettysburg when the turnpike was built in 1813.

Before the Battle of Gettysburg, the Cashtown Inn's innkeeper at the time, Jacob Mickley, witnessed the arrival of the Confederate army, saying: "The entire force under Lee passed within twenty feet of my barroom."

But it is from its use as a field hospital after the battle that the Inn gets its haunted lore. Amputated limbs were reported to be piled so high that sunlight could not enter.

Now used as a Bed and Breakfast, guests report hearing footsteps in their room along with frequent knocking at their door.

The Cashtown Inn has been visited by paranormal investigators and ghost-hunters, and was even featured on a Ghost Hunters episode.

The Cashtown Inn is located at 1325 Old Route 30, Orrtanna, PA.

The Gettysburg Academy B&B

The Gettysburg Academy Bed and Breakfast is one of the oldest and most historic buildings in Gettysburg, and has just begun to document its haunted activities. Built in 1813, the Academy got its name from being an educational facility in Gettysburg for more than 200 years.

The building was also used as a Civil War hospital after the Battle of Gettysburg. Bearing witness to its historic past is a student's signature that remains imprinted on an upstairs wall, as well as an artillery shell that is still lodged in its bricks.

There are ghost investigations carried out in this building, especially during Halloween.

The Academy is located at 66 West High Street.

The Historic Farnsworth House

The Farnsworth House Inn is a great place to eat, enjoy a cold beverage — and perhaps feel a chill since it is one of the most haunted places in Gettysburg.

This building was once used as a hospital after the Battle of Gettysburg, and it now serves as a restaurant and bar, bed and breakfast, and a top Gettysburg ghost hunting site.

From the cellar to the attic, the Farnsworth House is sure to set your spine tingling. The cellar offers a "Mourning Theater" complete with an antique coffin, and an upstairs window is believed to be where a sharpshooter took the fatal shot that killed Jennie Wade.

Visitors to this historic bed and breakfast tell stories of hearing strange noises emanating from the attic and singing coming from the basement.

Many tours are offered at the Farnsworth House as well as special ghost investigations.

The Farnsworth House is located at 401 Baltimore Street, Gettysburg.

The Dobbin House

The beautiful stone Dobbin House has been around for so long, it's almost impossible to think that a few supernatural spirits don't still walk the halls.

Not only did it witness the Battle of Gettysburg and its aftermath as a hospital, it was a stop on the Underground Railroad.

The building has a "secret room" where slaves were once hidden, and according to local lore, blood splatters mysteriously appear and disappear on the floor.

Now used as a fine dining restaurant, a pub and a bed and breakfast, the Dobbin House continues to host the spirits of former slaves who some visitors have seen meandering through the building.

Local ghost tour participants, and even a television crew, have reported seeing a young, frightened girl looking out the window.

Pro Tip: The Springhouse Pub is a great place to grab a bite to eat.

The Dobbin House Tavern is located at 89 Steinwehr Avenue, Gettysburg PA.

Haunted Sachs Covered Bridge

This Is One Of The Most Haunted Places In Gettysburg

Covered bridges can conjure an image of the charming times of the past, but the Sachs Covered Bridge has a history of ghostly encounters and is considered to be one of the most haunted places in Gettysburg.

Crossed by the retreating Confederate Army, the bridge is also said to be the site of the public hanging of three army deserters. Those who visit the bridge tell stories of seeing apparitions, smelling cigar smoke, hearing voices, and feeling a touch – when no one is there.

To learn more, see my full post with pictures and videos of the haunted Gettysburg covered bridge.

The Sachs Covered Bridge is located on Water Works Road.

The Gettysburg Hotel

The Gettysburg Hotel is located right on Lincoln Square and is a four-star hotel with a restaurant and bar/lounge.

Its history stretches back to 1797, when it began as a small tavern. During the 1890s, the property changed hands and the new owner decided to replace the old tavern with an imposing structure and named it the Gettysburg Hotel.

The most well known spirit to roam the halls of the Gettysburg Hotel is Rachel, who was reportedly a nurse during the Battle of Gettysburg. A Union soldier who died in the hospital is also seen wandering around.

Not well known is the fact that the hotel was once a bank, and a vault is still located in the ballroom. During a paranormal investigation that I attended, the vault was discovered to be the most haunted place in the rooms we investigated.

No one unearthed any findings of who died in the vault, but it is a spooky place to visit!

The Gettysburg Hotel is located at 1 Lincoln Square, Gettysburg PA

Pennsylvania Hall At Gettysburg College

Gettysburg College served as a field hospital for both Confederate and Union soldiers during the Civil War and has a long history of hauntings.

One of the most terrifying ghost stories I have ever heard as a Gettysburg local is from Mark Nesbitt's book Ghosts of Gettysburg.

He said that two college employees entered an elevator, pushed the button for their desired floor, and ended up in the basement. When the elevator doors opened, the women saw a bloody Civil War operating room with doctors working feverishly to save injured and dying soldiers.

As a doctor walked toward them, the elevator began to move to another floor. The two employees fetched a security guard and returned to the basement, but there was nothing out of the ordinary.

You can definitely see why this is on the list of the most haunted places in Gettysburg!

Gettysburg College is located at 300 North Washington Street, Gettysburg PA

Homestead Orphanage

Atrocities To Children Makes This A Top Haunted Place In Gettysburg

The Girl's Dorm of the Homestead Orphanage is now home to Civil War Tails at the Homestead museum, which I highly recommend if you are interested in seeing the Battle of Gettysburg and other engagements of the Civil War from a unique perspective.

During the Battle of Gettysburg, the Homestead was used as a headquarters for Union General Howard, however, that's not why it is haunted.

In 1866 it was turned into an orphanage and at one time housed 130 boys and girls!

Rosa Carmichael, the head mistress, was infamous for her cruelty and was even convicted of child abuse later on.

The orphanage closed in 1877, but either the dark spirit of Rosa — or some of the tortured children — are said to lurk in the basement.

The Homestead Orphanage is located at 758 Baltimore Street Gettysburg, PA.

Devil's Den And The Triangle

This is an interesting place to visit whether you're ghost hunting or just want to see a very historic site is Devil's Den and nearby Triangular Field.

Apparitions of Confederate sharpshooters have been sighted by the rocks at Devil's Den, as well as loud reports of "rebel yells," drumbeats and moaning.

I have heard numerous stories from locals driving through this section of the battlefield at night and seeing Civil War soldiers appear. Living in the area, many of them think it is just reenactors out for a stroll — until these figures disappear from sight in the blink of an eye.

I can also personally attest to my camera refusing to function at Triangular Field. This seems to be a common problem.

Sometimes the camera will work, but pictures are blank, and sometimes the batteries are suddenly dead.

This is a spooky place!

Devil's Den is located on Sickles Avenue, Gettysburg PA.

Battlefield Brew Works

'Spirits' Galore At This Haunted Place In Gettysburg

Located in a barn that was used as a Civil War hospital, Battlefield Brew Works is the perfect spot to go for a drink or a bite to eat after your ghost hunting excursions throughout Gettysburg.

You just might find another ghost!

During the Battle of Gettysburg, more than 1,300 soldiers were taken to the property. In fact, because of its location, the barn became one of the largest Confederate field hospitals in the area.

When the Confederates retreated after the battle, they left 446 soldiers at the farm for another 28 days.

Many of the wounded left behind were near death or were too seriously injured to be moved, and in fact, 47 men who on the farm were buried there. They were later re-interred in Hollywood Cemetery in Richmond, Va.

If you're a woman and don't usually need to take a friend with you to the restroom, you might just think again at Battlefield Brew Works. Find a partner because the ladies bathroom is the most haunted spot in the building!

Whether you come to taste some fine craft beers, grab a bite to eat, or explore their selection of "spirits" – you won't be disappointed with a visit to this historic barn.

Battlefield Brew Works is located at 248 Hunterstown Road, Gettysburg PA.

The Shriver House

The Shriver House Museum does a wonderful job of showcasing the civilian experience during and after the Battle of Gettysburg. Every room is set up the way it was in 1863, as if time has stood still.

The house was occupied throughout the Battle of Gettysburg, and used as a hospital afterward. The attic of the house was also used by Confederate sharpshooters. Forensic tests on the stains in the attic prove them to be human blood, supporting reports that at least two Confederates died there.

Among other discoveries during the house renovations were live rounds from the Civil War and a child's shoe. There are also numerous bullet holes that scar the brick on the outside.

Medical supplies were found hidden in the house during renovations as well, attesting to the fact that the home was used as a hospital.

If you don't make it to the Shriver House for Halloween 2022, the museum tour is popular on Thanksgiving Day and over the Christmas holiday season.

One of the owners of the Shriver House wrote a book about the family of George and Nettie Shriver who occupied the house during the Civil War. The Shriver's Story is a great read if you're interested in learning more about the history of the house and its occupants.

The Shriver House Museum is located at 309 Baltimore St. Gettysburg PA

Ghost Tours/ Paranormal

There are plenty of ghost tours to choose from in Gettysburg. Please call ahead, because these businesses change quote often.

There are some tours that walk the streets, some that take you on car tours, and some that visit buildings that were used as Civil War hospitals.

Be aware that you must book early during certain times of the year. Also some are seasonal so check before you go.

You can also read these posts on www.pastlanetravels.com for more information:

THE TOURS

Farnsworth House Ghost Walks
Lots of different tours available at this restaurant, pub and B&B.
401 Baltimore Street
717-334-8838

Gettysburg Ghost Tours and Paranormal Association:
47 Steinwehr Avenue, Gettysburg, Pa.
717-338-1818

Mark Nesbitt's Ghosts of Gettysburg Candlelight Tour:
271 Baltimore Street, Gettysburg, Pa.
717-337-0445

Ghostly Images Tour

(Walking tours, Jennie Wade Tour, Haunted Orphanage Tour, Ghost Bus Tours, Specialty Tours, Paranormal Investigations
778 Baltimore Street, Gettysburg, Pa.
1-877-680-8687

Haunted Gettysburg Tours / Haunted Gettysburg Paranormal Society

27 Steinwehr Avenue, Gettysburg, Pa.
717-253-5013

Civil War Ghosts

Tours meet at the front yard of Brickhouse Inn B&B
452 Baltimore St., Gettysburg, Pa
1-844-757-5657

Romantic Things To Do In Gettysburg

If you're looking for a romantic weekend getaway, Gettysburg is the perfect destination. From lovely restaurants and charming B&Bs to history-filled attractions and scenic drives, there are plenty of things to do in this picturesque town with your significant other.

Romantic Things To Do For History Lovers

This is a great place to start since there are SO many romantic things to do in Gettysburg PA for history lovers. I'll start with an absolute favorite, which is to visit Little Round Top at sunset.

There is nothing more romantic than sitting on such hallowed ground and taking in the vast painted sky with your loved one. It is breathtaking and beautiful, and will make memories that will last a lifetime.

NOTE: Little Round Top is closed for rehabilitation in 2023.

Of course, if you're a history lover, you're going to want to go to the Gettysburg National Military Park and Visitor Center and learn about what all there is to see in this historic Pennsylvania town.

The Gettysburg Visitor Center has a large bookstore and gift shop where you and your sweetheart can spend hours if you have the time.

Unfortunately, you probably won't, because you're going to want to visit at least one or two of the museums downtown. For those whose significant others may not be interested in the battle itself, try one that tells the interesting stories of civilians during the Battle of Gettysburg.

The Gettysburg Heritage Center and The Shriver House Museum are two that fill this bill.

Romantic Things To Do For The Adventurous

There are plenty of romantic things to do in Gettysburg for the adventurous as well. How about booking a Gettysburg Horseback Tour to experience the battlefield just the way they did back in 1863? (See Tours by Horseback section).

There are plenty of scenic horseback tours to choose from.

If your significant other is creative or likes solving puzzles, check out the 1863 Escape Room. Whether you're a history buff or a pure novice, the Escape Room is good for anyone who love a fun challenge.

If you want to treat your special someone to a spectacular view, climb one of the three battlefield observation towers in Gettysburg.

The towers are:

Oak Ridge Observation Tower located on Oak Ridge, north of Gettysburg. At only 23 feet tall, this tower is half the size of the other two, but offers panoramic views. Because of its location, it's good for both sunrises and sunsets.

Confederate Avenue Observation Tower is 75 feet high and provides great views of Pickett's Charge and the Round Tops.

Culp's Hill Observation Tower is 60 feet high is located southeast of the borough. The view is somewhat restricted during the summer months due to tree foliage.

Romantic Things To Do For Nature Lovers

There is no limit to the romantic things to do in Gettysburg, PA for those who love the outdoors and nature.

One thing visitors love to do is hike to the top of Big Round Top, a major landmark of the Gettysburg Battlefield.

It is less than a mile up to the top, but the incline is fairly steep, so wear comfortable shoes and bring water in the summer. This trail is great for birding, hiking and finding solace with nature.

You'll need a place to relax after your hike. What could be more romantic than enjoying time in the outdoors together by camping in Gettysburg? Lucky for you, there are plenty of options for camping near Gettysburg National Park.

Whether you want to pitch a tent, take your RV or book a romantic cabin in the woods, you'll find plenty of romantic opportunities in Gettysburg. (See Campgrounds section)

If you'd rather drive than walk, take a scenic road trip to see the apple, cherry and peach orchards just north of Gettysburg.

In the spring, the view is spectacular with miles and miles of orchards in full bloom. In the fall, you will see trees laden down with a wide variety of apples.

While you're out touring, stop at the Historic Gettysburg Round Barn for some fresh fruit or apple cider.

Romantic Things For Those Who Just Want To Relax

If you're looking for the most romantic things to do in Gettysburg that are relaxing, you can start with a Gettysburg horse drawn carriage tour and listen to the clip-clop of horses hooves hitting the pavement.

When you're done taking in the charm of this small historic town, you can head to the Gettysburg National Military Park, spread a blanket under a tree and enjoy a picnic.

With almost 6,000 acres of pastoral landscapes, forested knolls and gently-running streams, there are plenty of places for both the historian and nature-love to enjoy some quiet time.

At the end of the day, you can head to a historic B&B like the Gettysburg Academy or any of the other Gettysburg Bed and Breakfasts that are located in historic homes.

Gettysburg boasts a wide array of elegant and comfortable lodging in downtown Gettysburg, as well as large farmhouses out in the country. Some of the B&Bs were used as Civil War hospitals during the Battle of Gettysburg, so be prepared for "unusual encounters."

Romantic Things For "Foodies" In Gettysburg

If your idea of romance involves food and drink, you won't have any problem finding the perfect place to entertain your partner. In fact you can even book a savory Gettysburg food tour if you want to sample different cuisines.

If you'd rather go it alone, the Inn at Herr Ridge is a historic bed-and-breakfast that also boasts an excellent restaurant as well as a more casual pub that is located in an adjacent barn.

The Farnsworth House Inn is another great option for a romantic candlelit dinner with a historic atmosphere. The inn is located in a beautiful historic home, and the restaurant has an intimate, cozy feel.

For something a little more casual, check out Battlefield Brew Works, which is located in a barn that was used as a Civil War Hospital. (And is reportedly haunted).

If you want to take your honey to Gettysburg's "best kept secret," you have to try out Reliance Mine Saloon, better known as the "Mine Bar" to locals.

And for those who want to taste the local harvest through liquid refreshment, try the Adams County Pour Tour.

All you have to do is grab a passport and get it stamped as you treat you and your sweetheart to the wide variety of wines, ciders, spirits, meads and craft brews available in the Gettysburg area.

You can download an interactive trail map that allows you to plan your journey and get step-by-step directions to your next destination right from your mobile device.

The area surrounding Gettysburg is an agricultural paradise, with bountiful orchards, vineyards and farmlands that allow the creation of some amazing craft beverages.

Romantic Things To Do For Ghost Hunters

In addition to drawing history lovers, Gettysburg is also a magnet for ghost hunters—for good reason!

This small town is said to be home to some of the most haunted places in America, and it's the perfect place for a ghost lover's getaway.

If you're looking for a spooky tour that will have your significant other holding on tight, don't miss the Ghost Tours section.

There are lots of ghost hunting opportunities available in Gettysburg, including a Beginner's Evening Paranormal Investigation or an in-depth Paranormal Investigation.

This tours give you the opportunity to learn about the history of the town and the ghosts that haunt it. And you may even see a ghost or two!

If you're looking for spooky Civil War stories, then you need to check out Ghosts of the Civil War Haunted Walking Tour.

Yes, you can use their ghost hunting equipment and try to communicate with the ghosts of Gettysburg. It's the perfect way to get up close and personal with the paranormal!

Of course, no ghost hunting experience in Gettysburg would be complete without a visit to the Gettysburg battlefield. This historic landmark is said to be one of the most haunted places in America, and is great to explore on your own.

If you want some help, you can use this self-guided ghost themed tour.

If you're lucky, you'll be in town when the Daniel Lady House is open. In addition to Sachs Mill Bridge, it's one of the most haunted places in Gettysburg.

Romantic Things To Do In Gettysburg For Shoppers

Shoppers are in luck because no matter what your taste or style, there are plenty of romantic things to do in Gettysburg PA for shoppers.

From window shopping at the unique downtown stores to the Outlet Shoppes at Gettysburg, located just south of town, you and your sweetheart can spend hours holding hands and looking for that perfect "something."

If you enjoy antiquing, Gettysburg is only 11 miles from the small town of New Oxford, which is known as the Antiques Capital of Central Pennsylvania.

If you want to stick to Gettysburg, you can visit two of my favorites: The Antique Center of Gettysburg (lots of Civil War items) or Rebel's Roost which is located in a restored period barn on Rt. 30, east of Gettysburg.

If you want to combine your shopping with a museum, check out the Gettysburg Heritage Center. They have lots of Gettysburg battle information, Civil War artifacts AND a fantastic gift shop with lots of free parking.

Wrap-Up Of The Most Romantic Things To Do In Gettysburg

If you're looking for romantic things to do in Gettysburg PA, you've definitely found the perfect destination to cozy up with the one you love.

From its charming bed and breakfasts to its awe-inspiring history, there's something for couples of all interests in this small town.

Make sure to plan your visit ahead of time so you can take advantage of everything Gettysburg has to offer! The anniversary of the Battle of Gettysburg is July 1, 2 and 3, so that is a particularly busy part of the season.

Remember, whether you're a young couple just getting to know each other or you have been married for years, Gettysburg offers plenty of romantic things to do.

"Nothing Is More Romantic Than Sharing A Strong Passion With The Person You Love And Experiencing It Together."

– Larisa Moran Chancellor

Parking in Gettysburg

Parking can be hard to find during the busiest times of the year. There is on-street metered parking and the parking lots listed below. Check with the Parking Department for current rates.

You heard it from a local: The Parking Department is very vigilant. Pay the meters.

Borough Lot 1: 1st block of East Middle Street south side, this lot provides twenty four 3-hour parking meters.

County Lot: Located in the 1st block of East Middle Street north side, this lot provides 12-hour meters.

Parking Garage on Race Horse Alley off Stratton Street.

Reenactments in Gettysburg

A unique way to learn history is by witnessing battle re-enactments and by talking to those who immerse themselves in the past.

There is a reenactment every year in Gettysburg on the weekend closest to the date of the actual battle (July 1, 2, 3), with a larger event held on the anniversary years.

Not only do you get to see demonstrations of battlefield tactics and watch a mock Civil War battle, you can also wander through the encampments and talk to the soldiers about their daily life, clothing and firearms.

There are church services, demonstrations, book signings and talks, so arrive early!

Note: 2023 marks the 160th Anniversary of the Battle of Gettysburg.

THERE ARE TWO CIVIL WAR REENACTMENTS in 2023.

The annual event at the Daniel Lady Farm is slated for June 30, July 1 and July 2, 2023.

Where Is The Gettysburg Reenactment Held?

The Daniel Lady Farm, located at 1008 Hanover Road, Gettysburg, hosts the annual reenactment as well as numerous other special events throughout the year.

The house and barn are beautifully preserved and served as field hospitals during the Civil War. The farm is owned and managed by the Gettysburg Battlefield Preservation Association. https://www.gbpa.org/

Bleachers are being set up this year for better viewing by spectators.

Phone: 717-778-7760

Tickets for one day range from $15 to $35.

A three-day package runs from $40 to $100.

A Second Reenactment is being planned this year by another non-profit organization to help raise funds for endangered battlefields

The Patriots of the Civil War Association reenactment will be held June 23-25.

Historical talks, demonstrations and battles.

Location: 1289 Blackhorse Tavern Road, Gettysburg PA

Tickets are $25/day or $40 for a 2-day pass and $60 for a 3-day pass.

$6 for parking to help with the recovery of the fields.

For Information: info@thepcwa.org

Attending A Reenactment

Dress comfortably and wear walking shoes. Parking is in fields and requires walking to get to the site. Camps are spread out across many acres.

Pennsylvania is hot and humid in June and July. Wear light-colored clothing, bring water, sun block and hats. Hydrate before you arrive and stay hydrated.

Traffic can be an issue, so plan to arrive early!

The event features daily battle reenactments, usually narrated. You can also walk through encampments, see demonstrations, and shop at "sutler" stores. Food vendors available.

LIVING HISTORY IN GETTYSBURG

For living history encampments and talks throughout the year check the Gettysburg National Military Park site.

Interesting Places Close By

Historic Round Barn & Farm Market
Farm market in historic Round Barn.
298 Cashtown Road, Biglerville Pa.
(8 miles west of Gettysburg off Rt. 30.)
717-334-1984

Hanover Shoe Farm
2310 Hanover Pike, Hanover, Pa.
Large Standardbred horse breeding farm east of town.
Fields of foals in the spring/early summer.
717-637-8931

Land of Little Horses
125 Glenwood Drive, Gettysburg, Pa.
Get up close to miniature horses and other animals.
Shows daily. Great for kids.
717-334-7259

New Oxford Antique Shops
Small, historic town 13 miles East of Gettysburg
Lots of antique shops and historical buildings.
Antique Market and Craft Show each June.

Mother Seton Shrine
Promotes the life of the first native-born U.S. Saint.
Beautiful gardens and museum.
339 S. Seton Avenue, Emmitsburg, Md.
301-447-6606

Eastern Museum of Auto Racing
Open wheel, sprint cars, midgets, and stock cars to motorcycles, Indy cars, NASCAR, drag racing and more.
100 Baltimore Road, York Springs, Pa.
(10 miles North of Gettysburg)
717-528-8279

Mr. Ed's Museum
Elephant museum, toys, unique gifts, candy and roasted nuts.
6019 Chambersburg Road, Orrtanna, Pa.
(12 miles west of Gettysburg)

Other Landmarks In Gettysburg

Evergreen Cemetery: Burial site of John Burns, James Getty & Jennie Wade. Bronze statue of Elizabeth Thorn who buried many of the dead from the battle while six months pregnant.
799 Baltimore Street, Gettysburg
717-334-4121

Gettysburg National Cemetery: Site of Lincoln's speech, and final resting place of many Civil War dead. Taneytown Road for parking.
1195 Baltimore Pike, Gettysburg

Eisenhower's Farm: Tour President "Ike" Eisenhower's home and farm. Entry off of Baltimore Pike. Follow signs for parking. Varying hours and days depending on the season, but house tours are available throughout the summer on Thursdays, Fridays, Saturdays and Sundays. There are also special programs.
877-874-2478

The George Spangler Farm Civil War Field Hospital: Only accessible by shuttle bus from the Gettysburg National Military Park Museum and Visitor Center. Tickets must be reserved at the Visitor Center. Only open during summer months.

Local Special Events

There is always something going on in Adams County, so make sure you check with Destination Gettysburg for information when you are visiting. Here are a few of the highlights:

Bluegrass Festival: May & August at Granite Hill Campground. Top names in bluegrass.
www.gettysburgbluegrass.com

Gettysburg Bike Week: The second week of July. Thousands of motorcycles visit the town. The Bike Parade through the square is worth seeing. Keep in mind hotels fill up early.

National Apple Harvest Festival: First two weekends in October. 10 miles NW of Gettysburg.
www.appleharvest.com

Gettysburg Christmas Festival: First weekend in December. Activities throughout the town. Fun, festive atmosphere.

Gas Up Before Gettysburg

Helpful Hint: Because Gettysburg is a tourist town, gas prices are typically above or right at the national average. If you are coming from the South, gas up before you get into town.

Emmitsburg, Md, just six miles south of Gettysburg, often has gas prices that are 10 to 20 cents (or more) per gallon lower because of state taxes.

There is one gas station in Gettysburg that still pumps your gas if you don't want to get out of your car. It is only two blocks off the beaten path, but takes CASH ONLY.

Direct To You is located at 144 West Street (at the intersection of W. High Street and West Street).

Note: There is a beer distributor located right next door and a Right Aid Pharmacy is located across the street.

Speaking of Alcohol

If this is your first visit to Pennsylvania, you will find that the Commonwealth's liquor laws are unlike most other states.

The state government controls all liquor sales, and until recently, beer could only be bought by the case at a distributor, or at a bar.

There are two beer distributors in Gettysburg:

High Street Brews, 219 W. High Street, Gettysburg

Beer Mart, 1275 York Road (near the state store)

Wine and spirits, for the most part, are still only available through a "State Store" or at a winery or distillery of which there are plenty in Gettysburg.

The State Liquor Store, where you can buy all types of liquor is called Fine Wine and Great Spirits and is located at 1275 York Road (in the strip mall across from Wal-Mart)

One other place to purchase Beer and Wine is at the Giant store, right off the York Road at 44 Natural Springs Road.

Mead, Beer, Wineries, Distilleries, Cider

The gentle sloping hillsides surrounding Gettysburg are great for growing grapes for wines. In addition, Gettysburg produces craft beers, mead, spirits and cider. (Not a complete list)

Adams County Winery is the fifth oldest operating winery in Pennsylvania.
The Winery: 251 Peach Tree Road, Orrtanna, Pa.
Wine Shop: 25 Chambersburg St., Gettysburg, Pa.
Buddy Boy Winery Tasting Room
777 Baltimore Street, Ste 112, Gettysburg, Pa.

Hungry Run Wine Cellars offers sweet to dry and red to white.
619 Baltimore Street, Gettysburg, Pa.
717-420-5634

Reid's Orchard & Winery
http://www.reidsorchardwinery.com
2135 Buchanan Valley Road, Orrtanna
717-677-7047

Brookmere Winery
Small family winery
2 Lincoln Way East, New Oxford
717-479-5899

J & P Winery
More than 40 varieties of wine from sweet to dry.
48 Baltimore Street, Gettysburg
717-549-2513

Halbrendt Vineyard and Winery
Small family-owned winery
7 miles west of Gettysburg specializing in artisan wines.
1150 Evergreen Way, Orrtanna
717-334-7784

Craft Beer Breweries and Mead

Dawg Gone Bees
Honey and Mead.
430 Baltimore Street, Gettysburg
223-255-2275

Appalachian Brewing Company
Small-batch craft beer, craft soda and brewpub food.
259 Steinwehr Avenue, Gettysburg
70 Presidential Circle, Gettysburg

Tattered Flag Tap Room
Veteran-owned business with award winning beer, spirits and hand-crafted cocktails.
45 Steinwehr Avenue, Gettysburg
717-398-2193

Chicken Hill Distillery
Elk County distillery that expanded into Gettysburg at the outlet shoppes.
1863 Gettysburg Village Drive, Suite 520, Gettysburg
223-255-2174

Mount Hope Winery

Sample hand-crafted Mount Hope Wines, Swashbuckler Beers, Lancaster County Ciders and Spirits Distilling Company spirits.
19 Lincoln Square
717-677-2580

Boyer Cellars

A variety of traditional red, white and fruit wines and hard ciders. Tasting bar, ample seating, wrap-around porch and scenic views.
405 Boyer Nursery Road, Biglerville
717-446-1623

Reid's Winery and Cider House

Wine tasting, hard cider sales, live entertainment.
400 Baltimore Street, Gettysburg
717-334-7537

Thirsty Farmer Brew Works

Small batch family brewery with craft beer and hard cider.
290 Cashtown Road, Biglerville.
717-334-3325

Jack's Hard Cider Tap Room

Pop-up Tap Room at Suite 420 Outlet Shoppes
1863 Gettysburg Village Drive, Gettysburg

Day Trips From Gettysburg

Gettysburg is close to everything!

Hershey Park: World-class amusement park. 40 miles.

Lancaster County: Tours of Amish farms, antiques, hand-made quilts.

Washington DC: Take rail from Maryland or drive. 90 minutes.

Inner Harbor Baltimore: Shopping, aquarium, historical sites. 90 minutes.

National Civil War Museum in Harrisburg: 40 miles N

Northern Virginia Vineyards: Lots of vineyards and wine tasting shops. Less than 2 hours.

Philadelphia: Lots of colonial history, museums and shopping. 3 hrs. East.

Other Local Tours

Crop Hop: Farms and markets that offer a variety of seasonal fresh fruits & vegetables, pick your own fruit and flowers, farm tours, cooking classes, fresh meats, hands-on experiences, entertainment and more.

Lesser Known Local Battlefields

Fairfield: Cavalry action. 8 miles West.

Monterey Pass: Museum SW of Fairfield. 14325 Buchanan Trail East, Waynesboro, Pa.
Great place for hiking and reading wayside markers.

Battle of Hanover: 15 miles East.

Hunterstown: 3 miles Northeast.

East Cavalry Field: East of Gettysburg.

Other Popular Nearby Battlefields

- Antietam
- Harpers Ferry
- Monocacy

Where To Eat In Gettysburg

Gettysburg is known for its history, not its restaurants, but here are a few food stops where the locals go. This is definitely not a complete list, and just because a restaurant is not listed here doesn't mean it's not delicious.

Restaurants come and go, but these have been around forever.

Ernie's Texas Lunch (100+ years old)
58 Chambersburg Street
Hot dogs, light fare, great breakfasts. Cheapest lunch in town!
717-334-1970

Lincoln Diner (Everybody's favorite)
32 Carlisle Street by the RR tracks.
Open 24 hours.
717-334-3900

Federal Pointe Grill (Formerly Dunlap's Restaurant)
90 Buford Avenue
Family style. Great prices.
717-334-4816

O'Rorke's (Hangout place for reenactors)
44 Steinwehr Avenue
Casual cuisine and Irish spirits.
717-334-2333

Savorhood (Formerly The Pike)
10 different food choices, taproom and bar. No cash.
985 Baltimore Pike.
717-334-9227

Tommy's Pizza (Locals love it)
A local favorite for 35 years.
105 Steinwehr Avenue
717-334-4721

Lincoln Square Bars/Restaurants

The Pub Restaurant and Bar: NW corner
717-334-7100

Blue and Gray Restaurant and Bar: SE corner
717-334-1999

Gettysburg Hotel: NE corner
717-338-5455

Ploughman Cider Tap Room: SW corner

Flying Bull Bar: Local hang-out ½ block from Lincoln Square
28 Carlisle Street

Gary Owen Irish Pub: Popular with locals. 2 blocks from square.
126 Chambersburg St.
717-337-2719

Recommended For Historic Value & Food

Dobbin House: 89 Steinwehr Ave., Gettysburg, Pa. Part of underground railroad. Local favorite for dining. 717-334-2100

The Mansion House 1757: 15 Main St., Fairfield, Pa. (about 8 miles west of Gettysburg) Old inn and restaurant as seen on the Travel Channel. 717-642-5410

Farnsworth House: 401 Baltimore St. Notice the bullet holes on side of building. 717-334-8838

Inn at Herr Ridge: 900 Chambersburg Rd., Gettysburg, Pa. Historic tavern along Rt. 30. Also restaurant and pub. 717-334-4332

Hickory Bridge Farm: 96 Hickory Bridge Road, Orrtanna, Pa. Homemade and family style in historic building. 717-642-5261

"When I left Springfield [to become President] I asked the people to pray for me. I was not a Christian. When I buried my son, the severest trial of my life, I was not a Christian. But when I went to Gettysburg and saw the graves of thousands of our soldiers, I then and there consecrated myself to Christ."

Abraham Lincoln

Campgrounds Near Gettysburg Battlefield

If you're looking for camping near Gettysburg National Park in Pennsylvania, you're in luck. There are a number of campgrounds near the Gettysburg battlefield and the town, and they offer lots of fun-filled and family-friendly amenities.

Whether you want to sleep in a tent, hook up your RV, or even stay in a cabin or cottage, you'll find the perfect campground for your Gettysburg getaway.

But don't wait to book your retreat! All of these campgrounds fill up, especially over busy holiday weekends during the summer.

Tips For Camping Near Gettysburg National Park

There is definitely a wide range of activities and accommodations at these Gettysburg campgrounds, so it really comes down to your personal preferences.

Some of these campgrounds are located a few miles outside of Gettysburg and some are practically on the Gettysburg battlefield.

All of the campgrounds are close to the Gettysburg National Military Park and none are more than a few miles from the Visitor Center.

Artillery Ridge Campground And Horse Park

For those looking for camping near Gettysburg National Park, you can't get much closer than Artillery Ridge Campground and Horse Park.

Billed as the "closest campground to history," Artillery Ridge is located upon the very grounds where the Union Artillery Reserve was placed during the Battle of Gettysburg. The campground is within walking distance to Gettysburg Battlefield trails, museums and monuments.

Family fun activities include fishing in a stocked catch and release fishing pond, miniature golf, heated swimming pool, and a large playground.

They also have areas for basketball, volleyball, cornhole and horseshoes, as well as a game room with billiards and bingo.

Artillery Ridge is a full-service facility offering more than 400 sites for RV camping, tent camping, cabin camping and equestrian camping along with equestrian day use.

Campsites are available with or without hookups and include primitive as well as full-service cabins that can accommodate 4 to 6 people..

Every site, whether basic, premium or secluded has a picnic table and fire ring and there is easy access to multiple bath houses.

This campground is pet friendly with a fenced area to let your dog run free. (It's so nice to travel to destinations where pets are allowed, isn't it?)

Artillery Ridge is the only campground in Gettysburg that offers overnight accommodations for horses. In addition to stalls, they have a warm-up riding arena and round pen, as well as open gate corrals.

If you don't have your own horse but want to take a Gettysburg horseback tour, you can book a horseback tour.

Location: 610 Taneytown Road, Gettysburg, PA 17325

717-334-1288

Granite Hill Camping Resort And Bed And Breakfast

Whether you come to relax, to experience the area's rich Civil War history or to enjoy the outdoors or great views, you will find something to make everyone in the family happy at Granite Hill Camping Resort and Adventure Golf.

This scenic 150-acre Civil War era farm is the largest campground in Gettysburg and has a mix of woodlands, tree-dotted meadows and grassy rolling hills.

With 300+ sites, visitors have the choice of staying in the bright sunshine — or relaxing in forested seclusion among tall trees.

Granite Hill offers everything from private tent sites to spacious pull-thru sites catering to the largest RVs and Big Rigs, as well as a wide range of options in group camping and rustic cabins in a wooded setting.

A pre-Civil War farmhouse at Granite Hill Campground near Gettysburg is used as a bed and breakfast.

This beautifully restored brick farmhouse dates back to the 1860's and stood witness to the Battle of Gettysburg as well as 150+ years of local history.

Granite Hill offers a wide variety of amenities, activities and camping near Gettysburg National Park.

It is conveniently located far enough away from the crowds and commotion of downtown, yet close enough to have easy access to everything.

Some of the amenities at Granite Hill include a swimming pool (renovated in 2021), paddleboat and kayak rentals on their lake, playgrounds, doggie park and fishing pond.

They also offer basketball, shuffleboard, sand volleyball,

horseshoes, and an arcade.

Adventure Golf at Granite Hill is like no other course on the East Coast. Overlooking Lake Lily, the course starts with an unusual waterfall and cascading streams from atop their own Stone Mountain.

The course offers varying elevations, architectural mounds and dramatic landscaping to complement the new state-of-the-art greens. Everyone in the family will enjoy playing on this course that includes subtle undulations, sand traps and water hazards.

If you're hungry after a round of golf, visit the campground's Red Shed Café. It serves breakfast, lunch, and dinner, and offers wine & beer.

Regularly scheduled activities at Granite Hill include games, crafts, hayrides, dances, bonfire socials, nature walks and ghost walks, all under the supervision of a full-time Activities Director.

Granite Hill is also home to the internationally acclaimed Gettysburg Bluegrass Festival that is presented twice every year in May and August.

Running since 1979, the Bluegrass Festival has as many as two dozen traditional and contemporary bluegrass artists during the course of the four-day event.

The Festival also includes informative and instructional presentations, band showcases, meet & greets, and jam sessions.

Granite Hill offers themed weekends, including "foodie weekends," and tours to Gettysburg and Washington, D.C.

Location: 3340 Fairfield Road, Gettysburg, PA 17325

717-642-8749

Gettysburg Battlefield Resort

Another campground that offers facilities near Gettysburg National Park is the Gettysburg Battlefield Resort.

Located adjacent to the Gettysburg battlefield, this resort also offers plenty of history as well as fun activities for the entire family.

Gettysburg Battlefield Resort sign and entrance, which offers camping near Gettysburg National Park.

On hot summer days, you can go swimming in their Olympic-size swimming pool, fish in a stocked lake or take the kids to the playground.

The Battlefield Resort also has shuffleboard, beach volleyball, horseshoes, corn hole and an arcade. Finish off your afternoon of fun with hand dipped local ice cream at the snack bar.

If you're visiting Gettysburg for the history, they have battlefield reenactment grounds on their site. And if you're visiting to get away from it all, they have wonderful nature trails to explore.

They also have other special features including an authentic farmhouse lodge, climate controlled bathhouses, a general store, laundry facilities, internet access, outdoor pavilion and modern cabins.

The Gettysburg Battlefield Resort has 264+ campsites and offers RV spaces, tents and cabins. Both pull-through and shaded campsites are available.

Location: 1960 Emmitsburg Road, Gettysburg, PA 1732

1-866-834-3969

Drummer Boy RV Camping Resort

Located just east of Gettysburg, Drummer Boy RV Resort combines the picturesque countryside of Gettysburg with modern amenities for enjoyable camping near Gettysburg National Park.

Their resort offers 95 acres of wooded campsites and rental units, and they have more than 400 sites available for seasonal and short term rental.

The rentals include 15 cabins, 36 cottages and 10 lofts with a range of amenities including themed weekends and organized activities.

Whether you want to rough it or prefer complete luxury, Drummer Boy can accommodate you.

Never thought of luxury at a campground? How about relaxing in the campground's whirlpool spa after a long day of sightseeing?

Drummer Boy campground also has two heated pools, one of which includes a 250-foot water slide.

If you get hungry and don't want to leave the site, this campground near Gettysburg National Park has a snack bar that offers a wide variety of hot and cold items.

They also have a well-stocked camp store that offers everything from groceries and ice cream, to battlefield inspired gifts and souvenirs, as well as RV and camping supplies.

You can match your skills with your kids in the game room that offers both video and arcade games, air hockey tables and a prize redemption machine. Or challenge them to a game of mini golf on the campground's course.

Drummer Boy Campground provides access to daily shuttle service to downtown Gettysburg. This campground is within minutes of battlefield tours, ghost walks and Gettysburg Military Park Visitor Center.

Location: 1300 Hanover Road, Gettysburg, PA 17325

877-570-2267

Round Top Campground

Round Top Campground is a spacious family vacation oriented campground near the Gettysburg Battlefield, just off Route 15 south of the town.

As its name suggests, it is located near the famous Big and Little Round Tops, where part of the Battle of Gettysburg was fought.

This resort's amenities include 288 camp sites and 29 cottages/cabins located in an immersive camping environment that includes hillsides and forest trees.

They also have an Olympic size swimming pool and kiddie pool, brand new miniature golf course, shuffleboard courts, outdoor pavilion, game room, playground, basketball court, horseshoes and volleyball.

Other amenities at this campground near Gettysburg National Park include a country store, newly renovated bathrooms and fun filled special weekend and holiday events.

Some of their special events include wine tasting, scavenger hunts, carnival games and pumpkin carving.

Round Top Campground is perfect for an overnight or extended stay as well as for family camping on a seasonal basis.

They have sites that include full hook-ups, and their deluxe cottage vacation rentals sleep up to eight and include full linens, appliances and kitchenware.

Location: 180 Knight Rd, Gettysburg, PA 17325

877-570-2267

KOA Gettysburg / Battlefield KOA

Located about five miles from Gettysburg, the Gettysburg KOA Campground gives campers easy access to modern amenities while being surrounded by nature.

No matter what your idea of "camping" is, KOA can provide accommodations for you.

From luxurious RV glamping to rugged tent sites, Gettysburg KOA offers something for every experience level and comfort need.

If you prefer cabin camping, Gettysburg KOA lets you enjoy a hassle-free experience with many of the luxuries you have at home.

What could be better than enjoying the peace and serenity of nature while getting a good night's sleep in a comfortable bed?

Tent campers at KOA can get a taste of authentic camping life with access to all the essential amenities.

If you want to explore the Gettysburg battlefield, bus tour tickets are sold from KOA or you can explore on your with a self-guided CD tour.

KOA offers a heated pool, nature trail, gem mine, bike rentals, shuffleboard, horseshoes, corn hole, life-size games and mini golf.

Your pet can also enjoy the pet playground.

A nightly movie provides an overview of the town and battle. Bus tours depart from this KOA for the Gettysburg Battlefield or Washington, D.C.

After a day of touring, relax at this quiet, naturally wooded campground. If you just want to stay on site, you can enjoy the heated pool, nature trail, fun-bike rentals, shuffleboard and mini golf.

Weekend entertainment includes living history encampments, Civil War stories, ghost walks, wine tasting and pancake breakfasts.

Location: 20 Knox Rd, Gettysburg, PA 17325

717-642-5713

Gettysburg Campground

You can enjoy a relaxing getaway at Gettysburg Campground, located just 3 miles from the heart of historic Gettysburg and the battlefield.

Bordered by Marsh Creek, this campground offers 200+ RV sites, cottages and cabins as well as a dedicated tent area.

With the tagline "Stay Where History Happened," the campground sits across from a Civil War field hospital and lies along the Confederate retreat route.

You can stay on site and enjoy the amenities, or explore the Gettysburg area and beyond.

Gettysburg Campground has both sunny and shaded RV and tent sites, and offers a variety of back-in and pull-thru sites.

This campground is located along the tree-lined banks of the peaceful Marsh Creek, so you can stay close to the water or pick a spot near the pool.

All RV sites are generously sized, level gravel or paved, and include a fire pit and picnic table.

For those who don't have an RV, Gettysburg Campground offers rustic cabins in the woods that sleep 4.

They also have fully furnished cottages that sleep 6, with one full or queen bed and two sets of bunk beds. The fully-equipped kitchenette includes a table and chairs.

Cool off in their swimming pool with a small covered pavilion, wade in the creek, or just sit by the water and fish.

Don't forget to stop by the camp store for ice cream on hot summer nights, or take a relaxing hay ride through the encampment.

Gettysburg Campground also offers a fun-filled 18-hole geometrically-arranged holes on artificial turf.

Other activities include sand volleyball, shuffleboard, basketball and horseshoes.

They also have a Recreation Hall for activities and events, and a game room for "kids" of all ages.

The little kids will enjoy the playground and furry companions can stretch their legs in the special dog walking area.

If you're low on supplies, the camp store offers firewood, ice, ATM machine, pet supplies, fishing supplies, groceries, gifts and souvenirs.

Location: 2030 Fairfield Road, Gettysburg, PA 17325

717-334-3304

Other Camping Near Gettysburg National Park

Conewago Campground: A family owned and operated campground located about 11 miles northwest of Gettysburg. Established in 1967 by the Cole Brothers, it is clean and quiet with no frills. Everyone comments on the polite and friendly management. The sites are spacious and shaded, with a stream and waterfall for cooling off.

Location: 1507 Narrows Road, Biglerville, PA 17307

(717) 677-8958

Caledonia State Park: Located about fifteen miles northwest of Gettysburg near South Mountain, and is one of four parks surrounding the mountain.

The park has an 18-hole golf course and a designated swimming pool with a water slide, plus a slow moving mountain stream for cooling off or fishing. The park also offers ten miles of trails.

There are a total of 184 tent and trailer sites spread throughout two campgrounds. The camping season begins on the second Friday in April and ends in December, after deer season.

Those who do not want to camp but want to stay at the park can enjoy the Caledonia Lodge available year-round.

Location: 101 Pine Grove Rd, Fayetteville, PA 17222

Pine Grove Furnace State Park: Less than twenty miles north of Gettysburg, and offers spectacular vistas of the mountains surrounded by the Michaux State Forest.

Unique features of this park include two mountain lakes and the Appalachian Trail Museum. Public beaches and swimming are available at both Fuller and Laurel Lakes.

Hiking paths in the park range in length from a fourth of a mile to six miles, and a part of the Appalachian Trail runs through the park. Bikers, boaters, anglers, swimmers, and wildlife lovers will enjoy all the activity options the park offers.

If you enjoy bird watching, this is the place to go. Make sure to take your binoculars during the spring and fall migration period.

Campsites come with easy access to electricity, water, toilets, and warm showers.

Each site offers a picnic table and a fire ring with access to a store for anything you may have forgotten. A few designated campsites allow pets for those who travel with their furry companions.

If you're not into camping, you can book the historic two-story Paymaster's Cabin.

Location: 1100 Pine Grove Rd, Gardners, PA 17324

Wrap-Up Of Camping Near Gettysburg National Park

You can make Gettysburg your home base by camping near Gettysburg National Park and taking day trips to other points of interest.

Gettysburg is centrally located to Hershey, Amish Country (and antique shopping) in Lancaster, Washington, D.C. and Baltimore.

It is also close to the Antietam battlefield, Monocacy and a host of other lesser-known Civil War battle sites.

As you can see, whether you have a large RV, prefer a simple tent, or want to stay in cottage or cabin, you can find your perfect getaway or home-away-from-home in Gettysburg.

The Story of Old John Burns

The story of old John Burns of Gettysburg is a local favorite that shows the pluck and the patriotism of the older generation at the time of the Battle of Gettysburg.

Burns was called "old" because was a veteran of the War of 1812, and was 69 when he ran off to help the Union army during the first day of the Battle.

The fire of patriotism obviously burned bright in John Burns of Gettysburg. Here is his story.

Old John Burns: A True Patriot In Gettysburg

John Lawrence Burns was not from Gettysburg originally. He was born in Burlington, New Jersey in September of 1793. In addition to serving in the War of 1812, Burns also served in the American-Mexican war.

Amazingly, he was 54 by the end of that war. (In 1860, the life expectancy was 39.4 years).

Nonetheless, Burns was a patriot and devoted to his country. When the Civil War broke out, despite being almost 68, he attempted to enlist in the Union army.

Needless to say, Burns was rejected, but was given the job of serving as a constable in Gettysburg.

When Confederate General Jubal Early arrived in Gettysburg, Burns resisted the Confederates' authority and was jailed. As the enemy troops departed, Burns was released from jail — but he didn't just sit around.

Instead, he went out and arrested any Confederate stragglers he could find.

Burns Defends Gettysburg

On the first day of the Battle of Gettysburg (July 1, 1863), John Burns heard the sounds of the battle. Grabbing his flintlock musket and powder horn, he told his wife, "I'm going to see what is going on."

Making his way toward the chaos of battle, Burns came across a wounded Union soldier. Since the soldier no longer needed his weapon, Burns asked if he could use the injured man's more modern rifle.

The soldier agreed and Burns moved on with the rifle, sticking the gun cartridges in his pocket.

When Burns found Major Thomas Chamberlin of the 150th Pennsylvania Infantry, he requested to be allowed to fall in with his troops.

Chamberlin later wrote of John Burns of Gettysburg:

"His somewhat peculiar dress consisted of dark trousers and a waistcoat, a blue "swallow tail" coat with burnished brass buttons, such as used to be affected by well-to-do gentlemen of the old school about 40 years ago, and a high black silk hat, from which most of the original gloss had long departed, of a shape to be found only in the fashion plates of the remote past."

Despite his skepticism about the request, Chamberlin referred him to the regimental commander, Colonel Langhorne Wister.

Colonel Wister sent the aged Burns into the woods next to the McPherson Farm, where he would find better shelter from the sun and enemy bullets.

John Burns Fights At Gettysburg

Anyone who knows about the Battle of Gettysburg realizes

that the McPherson Farm was the scene of intense fighting.

John Burns of Gettysburg ended up fighting with the famous Iron Brigade throughout the afternoon. In fact, he served as a sharpshooter, in one case shooting a charging Confederate officer from his horse.

But as the Union line began to give way and fall back to the Seminary, Burns received wounds in the arm, the leg, and even his breast. With their lines being overrun, the Union soldiers ended up leaving him behind on the battlefield.

Despite his injuries, the old man crawled away from his rifle and buried his ammunition. When the Confederates overtook the field and discovered him, he convinced them he was a noncombatant, seeking aid for his invalid wife.

The Confederates believed him and even had his wounds dressed by their surgeons.

This was a truly narrow escape. According to the rules of war, he was subject to summary execution as a non-uniformed combatant, otherwise known as a bushwhacker.

After having his wounds dressed, Burns crawled to the cellar of the nearest house later that evening, and was then conveyed to his own home.

John Burns Of Gettysburg Becomes Famous

As the story of John Burns' exploits at the Battle of Gettysburg began to spread, it captured the interest of famed photographer Mathew Brady.

Two weeks after the battle, Brady's assistant Tim Sullivan went to Gettysburg and photographed old John Burns.

Burns posed for the photo while recuperating in a rocking

chair, with a pair of crutches and a musket beside him, that is now famous.

John Burns Honored With Monument

The popularity of John Burns' participation in the battle grew in the post war years. His home on Chambersburg Street was razed after his death and veterans of the battle thought something should be done to commemorate his services.

A monument was eventually placed on the field where Burns had fought with the 150th Pennsylvania and 7th Wisconsin regiments, next to Herbst Woods.

Burns looks defiant, with a clenched fist, carrying his borrowed rifle.

Placed upon a boulder taken from the battlefield, the monument was dedicated on July 1, 1903, on the occasion of the 40th anniversary of the battle.

The tablet on the monument to John Burns reads:
My thanks are specially due to a citizen of
Gettysburg named John Burns who although
over seventy years of age shouldered
his musket and offered his services
to Colonel Wister, One Hundred and
Fiftieth Pennsylvania Volunteers.
Colonel Wister advised him to fight in the
woods as there was more shelter there
but he preferred to join our line of
skirmishers in the open fields. When the
troops retired he fought with the Iron
Brigade. He was wounded in three places."
-Gettysburg report of Maj.-Gen. Doubleday.

If you want to visit the monument to John Burns, it is located west of Gettysburg on the east side of Stone Avenue just south of Chambersburg Road (U.S. 30).

John Burns Buried In Evergreen Cemetery

Burns is buried in Evergreen Cemetery in Gettysburg, and is one of only two graves with permission to fly the American flag twenty-four hours per day. The other grave is that of Jennie Wade, the only civilian killed during the battle.

His original gravestone was vandalized, but replaced in 1902, bearing the inscription "Patriot."

The Battle of Gettysburg:

An Excerpt from the 'History of Adams County'

I'm including this excerpt from the "History of Adams County" so you can appreciate the struggle that occurred here and read a slice of history that isn't often talked about.

Jenkins' Cavalry galloped into Gettysburg the afternoon of the 26th of June. They took possession of the town and threw out their pickets. Early soon arrived, and his presence and words quickly assured the people that they were not to be seriously molested—that they were in no personal danger of harm. The rebels met, as they came in from different streets, at the triangle. They were tired, ragged, dirty and hungry, but evidently suffering more from long marches than anything else.

When permitted to stack arms, or put themselves at rest, they lay down on the sidewalks and in the streets with their knapsacks under their heads. When citizens would attempt to engage them in conversation, they were invariably silent.

Guards were posted about the public buildings and some of the stores, and a few, but very few, private houses. The saloons were closed without exception. Early was in command of trained soldiers, as is evidenced by the observance of his strict orders that the soldier was to molest neither person nor property of the inhabitants. And as an evidence of how rigidly orders were obeyed by these poor fellows, who had to go on guard duty about different places and premises, some of the women were excited in sympathy, and offered them something to eat, or water to drink, which was invariably refused, and, if asked why, they would curtly reply: "I must obey orders."

Early called the borough authorities to his presence, and he told them what he wanted of the borough: namely: 1,200 pounds of sugar, 600 pounds of coffee, 60 barrels of flour,

1,000 pounds of salt, 7,000 pounds of bacon, 10 barrels of whiskey, 10 barrels of onions, 1,000 pairs of shoes and 500 hats, or in lieu of all this $5,000 in cash.

[The men] replied that it was impossible to comply with the demand; that the goods were not in the town or could not be found; that the town had no funds; that the banks had shipped away their money and the people the most of their personal property, etc. No serious attempt was made to enforce the order further.

Effects Following the Battle

No portion of the northern states suffered equally with this part of Pennsylvania, or so to speak more clearly, with Adams County, in the late war. It was on the part of the people of his county more than any other county in the state—all sacrifices, losses, suffering, the general destruction of property and the total prostration of business, with no compensating advantages.

For three years during the five years of bloody contention, Adams County was virtually a part of the seat of war. Actually invaded three times and eventually the Waterloo of the great Southern army... In 1862, Stuart circled our army in his first, great northern raid, and his entire command passed up through the western part of this county.

After the Battle of Gettysburg and the armies had passed over the hills and away, they left the bloody debris of the great battlefield, the decaying bodies of unburied men and dead horses and a country swept bare of nearly everything, as the heritage of the citizens. And this and the maimed and dying on the hands of the charity of a people, who had really little except their labors to bestow in charity. The crops of the farmers of had been indiscriminately destroyed, fences were completely gone. The smokehouses were empty, so were the barns. And those who did not lose their stock were left with nothing to feed them... So completely were the farm fences destroyed that we were told you could start at Gettysburg and ride following any point of the compass to any part of the county unobstructed so far as any farm fence was concerned.

To all this the great tax upon the people of providing and caring for the wounded from the bloody battlefield of Gettysburg, and then in burying the dead that had been left lying where they fell. Rebel and Union lay rotting in the hot sun side by side. People threw open their private houses; the churches, the schoolhouses, the public halls, and even the barns and stables rang with the groans and agony of the shot, maimed and mutilated that filled apparently every place, and still the field of death and agony could yet furnish more victims.

The churches looked much as though they had been converted into butchers' stalls. The entire community became hospital nurses, cooks, waiters or grave diggers. In this wide expanse of Christian charity, rebel and Union sufferers were cared for without material distinction.

The Government ambulances commenced to carry away from the field their bleeding cargoes; soon every wheeled vehicle was at work bearing its loads of bleeding agony-filled with its pale sufferers garnered from the field where the cannon, the musket, the rifle and the saber had mowed their hideous swaths in living human ranks. Would these whirling wheels, in their quick trips back and forth as they dumped their loads of sufferers, never top?

What a swollen, great rushing river of agony! Literally half the surface of the entire county was a hospital, and every farmhouse, barn, stable, outbuilding, for twenty miles square, were full to overflowing. The beds, the floors, the yards, everywhere were they cared for, and behind them in the lines of battle, in the brush, by the side of the little spring streams where they had so painfully dragged themselves or sometimes been carried by their companions, were the uncollected dead and dying mostly.

What a ghastly harvest to gather from the fair and peaceful fields of Adams County. And when the poor bruised and maimed bodies were gathered in this widely extended hospital and laid side by side, what never-to-be-forgotten scenes were there.

The pale sufferers, the flushed, feverish and raving maniacs, whose reason had given way as they lay upon the field suffering, and watching the stars, and welcoming the storm and rain that came like pitying tears from heaven to soften their hardening, blood-clotted clothes, to moisten their horrid wounds and cool the raging fevers of their brows—Union and rebels, sons and fathers and brothers. Here the smooth-cheeked boy, the darling, the pet and home of home; there the lusty man, yesterday in the prime of life and strength, now in the midst of his suffering and pain...

These blue and gray, now so quiet, so friendly, so full of compassion for each other; and but a few hours ago, how they fought, how viciously they struggled to kill each other. Possibly the surgeons, who bound up these wounds, alone can someday tell the world how savagely men fought upon the bloody field of Gettysburg.

Death and convalescence began at once to lesson this great population of wounded, suffering patients, and the last of the patients form the tent hospitals, in the beautiful grove east of town, were moved away in the early part of November, 1863—over four months from the commencement of the Gettysburg battle.

Military Terminology

An army is the largest military unit, but strength varied considerably. The Confederacy had 23 such armies, each one usually taking its name from its state, and commanded by a full general, four stars.

A Corps is two or more division from 15,000 to 20,000 men. The South did not adopt this organization until after the time

A Division is made up of two or more brigades. If they were at full strength, 8,700 officers and men, commanded by a major general, two stars.

A Brigade is two or more regiments. The average confederate brigade was 4.5 regiments, roughly 1,850 men. Commanded by brigadier general, one star.

A Regiment is made up of 10 companies. With 1,000 and 845 men. Commanded by a colonel.

A Company was made up of about 100 men.

As the war progressed, numbers declined. A company was then made up of far less than at the beginning. New recruits formed new ones instead of going to others.

Dear Reader,

I hope you enjoyed this Visitors Guide to Gettysburg! If you have time, please leave a review!

And if you have any suggestions for improvement or additions, feel free to email me at:

writefromthepastATyahooDOTcom.

Happy Travels!

If You Like Historical Fiction...
Shades of Gray: A Civil War Novel
Award-winning Historical Fiction

Honor and conviction clash with loyalty and love in this epic Civil War love story that pits brother against brother. The Shades of Gray Trilogy chronicles the clash of a Confederate cavalry officer with a Union spy as they defend their beliefs, their country, and their honor.

What readers say about Shades of Gray...

"If you want to read a book you will never forget and will think about for months after reading it, read Shades of Gray. It took my breath away. Honestly, you will not sleep."

"My house is a mess, my sink is piled high with dishes and my husband ate watermelon for dinner because I could not put down Shades of Gray. Could. Not. Put. Down. Honestly, this book completely captivated me and left me emotionally drained. I loved it!!!"

"I've not been much of a reader and was given Shades of Gray. I've read it five times and fall in love every time I read it. Because of you I have developed a love for reading."

"It is now 1 a.m. cause I couldn't put down my I-pad with your delicious novel. Thank you for the pleasure you afforded this 81 year old."

"Wonderful, fabulous book! I seldom reflect back on a book, but this one has haunted me since I finished it at 2 a.m."

"Could hardly work or sleep until I read the last page."

"Lost a lot of sleeping reading this one. Too good to put down! Made me laugh. Made me cry. Awesome book!"

"I loved this novel. Still crying, but I laughed just as much as I cried."

"Bravo! One of the best books I have read on the Civil War. Absolutely could not put it down. Please do not stop writing."

"I can't remember having such a heavy heart and crying so much since reading Gone with the Wind. Thank you!"

"Loved. Loved. Needs to be made into a movie."

"I'm not usually one for Civil War era books, but I've got to say you really got me on this one. I LOVE it!"

"Oh my, I let the world go on around me and could hardly put it down. Every free moment, every break at work. LOVED IT!!!"

"I was completely lost and spellbound by the realistic story. Without hesitation I must say this now ranks equally with Gone With The Wind."

"Though a male I liked it, and recommended it to my wife."

"I stayed up until 2 a.m. two nights in a row because I couldn't put it down. It was a book that I couldn't wait to read, yet I didn't want it to end!"

"This book has touched me more than any other I have ever read. I cried, laughed, and then cried some more. Thank you for such an amazing and touching story."

"If someone said I could only ever have one book for the rest of my life Shades of Gray would be my pick. Thank you."

"I know a book is very good when I think about it after I complete the book, and I cannot start another one right away. Five star rating for sure."

"This book absolutely ripped my heart out. Superb. Thank you for such a moving, believable love story."

"I have not read a romance novel in probably 10 years. Your book was so good for my soul."

Professional Praise for SHADES OF GRAY

(Civil War Trilogy)

"It is a book that I think could have the impact of a 'Gone With the Wind.'"

– Jonathan A. Noyalas, Assistant Professor of History and Director for Civil War Studies, Lord Fairfax Community College

"Shades of Gray explores the War Between the States in a way that will touch you like no other work of fiction." – The Book Connection

"A fine addition to anyone's library of historical novels." – J.E.B. Stuart, V

"I think it is the best Civil War fiction book since Cold Mountain." – James D. Bibb SCV Trimble Camp 1836

"You cannot leave this book unchanged in your understanding of the souls of the Civil War." – Book Review Journal

Available everywhere books are sold.

Duty Bound

Honor Bound

Glory Bound

SHADES OF GRAY TRILOGY

About the Author

Jessica James is an award-winning author of fiction and non-fiction ranging from the Revolutionary War to modern day. She is a four-time winner of the John Esten Cooke Award for Southern Fiction and numerous other literary awards.

James' novels appeal to both men and women, and are featured in library collections all over the United States including Harvard and the U.S. Naval Academy.

She lives in Gettysburg, Pa.

Connect with her at jessicajamesbooks.com.

Join her newsletter and receive free content:

www.subscribepage.com/jessicajamesnews

Like History and Travel?

Join Jessica as she uncovers almost-forgotten history throughout the USA on her Past Lane Travels website.

www.pastlanetravels.com

Enjoy Reading Civil War Fiction?

Other Books by Jessica James

AWARD-WINNING WOMEN'S FICTION

LACEWOOD (Dual Era/Civil War)

AWARD-WINNING HISTORICAL FICTION

THE LION OF THE SOUTH

SHADES OF GRAY TRILOGY: Duty Bound, Honor Bound, Glory Bound

NOBLE CAUSE (Book 1 Heroes Through History)

ABOVE & BEYOND (Book 2 Heroes Through History)

LIBERTY & DESTINY (Book 3 Heroes Through History)

HEROES THROUGH HISTORY BOXED SET (Books 1-3)

AWARD-WINNING ROMANTIC SUSPENSE (Not Civil War)

PRESIDENTIAL ADVANTAGE

DEADLINE (Phantom Force Tactical Book 1)

FINE LINE (Phantom Force Tactical Book 2)

FRONT LINE (Phantom Force Tactical Book 3)

PHANTOM FORCE TACTICAL SERIES SET 1-3

PROTECTING ASHLEY

MEANT TO BE: A Novel of Honor and Duty

www.ingramcontent.com/pod-product-compliance
Lightning Source LLC
Chambersburg PA
CBHW060326050426
42449CB00011B/2678